"Here's Luck!"

"Here's Luck!"

By

Hugh Wiley

J. H. SEARS & COMPANY, Inc.
Publishers   New York

"HERE'S LUCK!"

COPYRIGHT, 1928, BY
J. H. SEARS & CO., INCORPORATED

COPYRIGHT, 1928, BY
THE LEGION PUBLISHING CORPORATION

MANUFACTURED COMPLETE BY THE
KINGSPORT PRESS
KINGSPORT, TENNESSEE
United States of America

TO THE
EIGHTEENTH ENGINEERS, A. E. F.

CONTENTS

CHAPTER		PAGE
1.	FALL IN!	1
2.	HEAVE HO!	37
3.	ENTENTE CORDIALE AND OTHER DRINKS	69
4.	FIRST TO FIGHT—FOR CUPID	109
5.	BIGGER AND BETTER UPLIFT	143
6.	FIFTEEN HUNDRED BUCKS	175
7.	THAT AIN'T NO LADY	217
8.	AS YOU WUZ!	259

"HERE'S LUCK!"

Chapter 1

FALL IN!

"A sound of Reveille by night!"

WAY deep in the Douglas Fir, Jimmy the Ink laid down four spades and answered the telephone.

He listened carelessly for a moment, and then, forgetting his four spades and the interrupted two-bit game, he wrapped his ear around the receiver and concentrated on the message that was coming in. He muffled the transmitter with the palm of his hand and turned to a player who was bearing up under three jacks: "Old King-pin wants to talk to you, Spike. Get on the line here. He seems all steamed up about something."

Spike Randall, roving grief-eater of King Timber, Inc., took the telephone from the camp timekeeper's hands and listened to the kindly voice of Phineas "Finish" King, czar of the local empire of industry. "Spike Randall speaking, Mr. King . . ."

"Twenty-four sticks, twenty by twenty, ninety feet long." "Finish" King's voice, filtering through a hundred miles of copper, seemed to vibrate with a resonance deeper than the occasion demanded.

"Twenty-four sticks, twenty by twenty, ninety feet," Spike Randall repeated.

"Listen, Spike. This stuff goes to the Atlantic coast on a silk-train schedule. Give it right of way over everything. The N. P. will spot your cars to-morrow. Get 'em loaded by to-morrow night, if it takes a thousand men. Win or lose, we're in the game now to the finish."

"What game?" Spike asked, thinking of his neglected three jacks.

"The Big Game, boy—the war with Germany. Washington just had me on the wire and I pledged my word this stuff would start east to-morrow night and catch a ship that sails Friday. Need it for some crane rigs to unload ships with in France. Million men to feed. Hit the ball."

Relaxing slightly with a sense of duty nobly performed, "Finish" King returned to his heavy poker at his club in Seattle. The two-bit game at Sky Timber was, however, busted wide open.

"This country's in the war on its own," Spike Randall explained, forgetting his three jacks. "Washington got the Old Man on long distance and yelled for some long stuff to use in France. Got to get it out by to-morrow. Twenty-four sticks, twenty by twenty, ninety feet long. Get Buck in here, Jimmy, and then roust out the cookhouse. Sky Timber hits the ball on a moonlight shift."

Jimmy the Ink put on his coat. "Damn them damn four spades! That hand might of been the first straight flush I ever held in my life, and here a damn war comes along and busts it up."

"You win the ante—grab it and run. Wake up those cooks. They'll never get rich asleep at the switch—they're in the Army now!"

Working with the system and energy that had made King Timber the biggest outfit of its kind in the world, Skyline Camp made the grade, and on Friday morning the special timber train which had raced across the continent ahead of the passenger schedules reached the Atlantic seaboard.

Here, suiting the purposes of the Finnegan Construction Company, who needed some good heavy timber for shoring a subway shaft, it was snaked out from under the eyes of a quartermaster sergeant nominally on duty in the interests of the U. S. A. Thereafter, lost to mortal view, it became one of a myriad Matters of Record.

Efficiency, fired by a slow fuse, finally blew up and King Timber cut an encore.

The second shipment, a duplicate of the first rush order, started east nine weeks later. This time, riding the train to guard it from further accidental detours, were Spike Randall and Jimmy the Ink.

Spike was equipped with a roll of bank notes for emergencies, but no emergencies were encountered until, in the clearing yards

Fall In!

at Chicago, a hard-boiled young yardmaster attempted to clear a trainload of structural steel ahead of the timber special.

"Where the hell do you get that stuff!" the vigilant Spike inquired, hearing the railroad man yell a clearance to the waiting crew of the steel train.

The yardmaster flagged Spike with a clenched fist from which fluttered the flimsy tissue documents from the dispatcher's office.

"You'll run second section, Extry 76," the railroad man barked.

"I'm running Extry 76, and if there's any second section to the drag it don't interest me a damn bit. Hand that 76 stuff to my train crew and git the hell out of my way!"

"Git calm, big boy, git calm!" The railroader backed up his polite request by reaching 'way back and low for a haymaker, which, delivered on time, staggered Spike to the roots of his back teeth.

"You son of a wreck!" Bam! Spike signed a receipt for the first wallop and dished out an encore before he felt a warm gush of blood spurting from the remains of his nose which seemed to have skidded up under his left eyelid.

Round one, a draw.

Round two, a draw. Not so much footwork.

In round three, detecting a flock of fouls, Jimmy the Ink stepped in with a short section of air hose. The assassin sapped the railroader once for the Honor of the Flag. He opened the inert man's clenched fist and retrieved the shredded train orders. He handed one of the yellow slips to the engineer of the timber train.

"Read it," he ordered. "Read it and hit the ball!"

He turned to the crew of the steel train. "You birds heard what this louse said"—indicating the inert yardmaster— "Well, tag along as the second section of Extry 76 if you crave to." Then, to Spike: "Pick up this mule's hind legs. We better take him along and doctor him up. I got so excited I might of socked him too hard. Let's go!"

Thirty minutes out of Chicago the battling yardmaster opened his eyes. "What time is it?" he asked. "Where are we?"

"Midnight, and headed east," Spike Randall answered through his battered and swollen lips.

"I remember now." The railroad man peered at Spike and in the dim light of the caboose Spike saw a smile on his adversary's lips. "We runnin' second section?"

"Your pet steel train is flyin' that flag."

"Fair enough. I know when I'm licked."

"Git to sleep, old-timer." Jimmy the Ink smoothed the folded coat under the yardmaster's head. "It took a blackjack earthquake to lick you."

"Orders is orders. Wake me up somewhere up the line soon enough for me to get back to Chicago by to-morrow night. That wallop gave me the first sleep I've had for five days, and I might as well get plenty while I'm at it. This war traffic has the train service all shot to hell, anyhow, and another little shot won't do it any harm."

"Speaking of shots"—Spike pulled a bottle of rich red likker out of his valise—"I've been saving this for emergencies. How about bustin' Rule G in the nose with a peace treaty?" He held out his right hand to the recumbent railroader. "Wild man, I'm sorry we had to mingle so violently."

"So am I. Forget it . . . Here's luck!"

Long before the S. O. S. meant "Sick of Salmon," a few civilian brains figured that the army was none too long on its supply of construction talent.

It is a fine thing to have a million men spring to arms overnight, provided they have the arms to spring to, plus ammunition.

It is gratifying to hungry men to hear a blister-lip bugler chortling through the first few verses of the Mess Call, provided the cooks can begin where the bugler leaves off. An army craves its groceries.

Sunny France is a beautiful land now and then, but in the moist and frigid intervals between sun spots a dash of wearing apparel, be it ever so porous and sketchy, is not to be scorned by those who prefer to retain their health and strength until they can shoot the works and spend it in a bunch.

Fall In!

Not long after the United States dashed in, after due deliberation, to draw cards in the Big Game, it became apparent that food and clothing and shelter might be desirable equipment for the millions who had, overnight, sprung to their phantom arms. Presently it appeared that time was the essence of America's contract with victory, and it was then that High Command began to question the ability of some of the penny-ante professionals who had drawn cards in the Big Game.

Members of the military nobility who had encountered some difficulties in supporting a wife and three children suddenly demonstrated their inability to provide for families of two or three hundred thousand.

In the midst of the tumult and the shouting, when frazzled fatheads had begun to trot with the right foot while standing on the left in military manner, the projected A. E. F. came to mean, in privileged minds, "All Efforts Futile." There seemed to be no doubt about Columbia, the Gem of the Ocean, being a diamond in the rough, but what the hour demanded was talent which could polish the Gem and insure its setting in the diadem of Victory.

It was then that Uncle Sam, fed up on fizzles, turned away from the gold-plated figureheads of the Ship of State, the scarecrows and the stuffed shirts which adorned the old homestead, to hunt up some new and vigorous hired men.

Answering the summons, emperors of industry smiled coldly and played brief overtures on pearl buttons mounted on the under edge of glass-topped desks. Steel and Timber, Agriculture and Transportation spoke quietly to attentive aides, and in a little while the mob of millions had exchanged their phantom arms for tangible tools of warfare.

The eastward march had begun, and in the van compacted almost overnight from sources ranging between two seas, were regiments of Engineers.

Somewhere along the line between Chicago and New York the kidnaped railroader had decided to make the rest of the run to New York with Spike and Jimmy the Ink.

"Every line out of Chicago is running hay wire, anyhow, with all these cuckoo orders balling up the traffic," the railroader reflected, and then to his two companions: "Sure I'll ride through with you. Kind of like to get an eyeful of New York, anyhow. I've been working days, nights and Sundays in the Chicago yards so long that I forget what a town looks like. Besides that I might be able to help you bust this timber through that tangle in the terminals up ahead."

"Now you're talkin' sense," Spike returned. "I'll be mighty glad to have your help at the finish. I've got to hunt up the local king snipe of the army quartermaster outfit and lay this timber right in his left hand while Jimmy gets a receipt for it out of the mitt he salutes with. Seventeen tracers on that first shipment and a hundred tons of letters have been fired back and forth between my outfit and the army brass necks. Nobody knows where it went to yet. Talk about the guy that lost the bass drum—looks like these old-timers in the army can pull a disappearing trick with a trainload of dimension stuff slicker than Jimmy can lose a pay check in a Seattle ruckus."

"I'll ride through with you," the railroad man repeated, "and we'll pull a three-man parade up and down Broadway before we start back. When we get in, you and me rides herd on this train till Jimmy locates your boss brass neck. Then we slams this timber into his left hand like you say, and after that —highball for the bright lights."

Much to the impatient Spike's delight, when the long trainload of timber had pulled into the terminal yards, Jimmy's scouting trip in search of the proper authority to receive the shipment lasted less than twenty minutes.

"He says cut her in two and back her down onto those two stubs at the long pier. The ship has been layin' there ever since noon waitin' for this stuff. She's the *Starvonia* and she's got a mob of Engineer soldiers on board."

"Fast work, Jimmy," Spike commended,

and then to the railroader, "See if you can get us a clearance through the yards."

"Highball in five minutes," the railroad man returned, and, true to prediction, within that time the timber train began to roll over the last mile of its eastward trip.

"Looks like the army is wakin' up." A reception committee of three or four hundred men waiting to unload the train inspired the comment from Spike.

"That fat bird up there with his coat on is the quartermaster colonel," Jimmy pointed out as the train halted near the long pier against which the *Starvonia* lay waiting. "He's the guy that can pardon us free from this watchman's job. Git his name on the receipts for these personally conducted fir slivers, and away we go."

So near and yet so far. "The terms of delivery specify that the timber in question shall be received by the Quartermaster Department, United States Army, on board ship," orated the quartermaster colonel. "I will sign those documents, young man, just as soon as your contract is fulfilled as specified, and not before."

Click!

Up against granite and realizing it, Spike accepted the terms. "Very well, Colonel—how long will it take your outfit to transfer the timber to the ship?"

"About three hours, sir. I will sign your receipts at five o'clock."

Good old beer. That was the thought uppermost in the minds of Jimmy the Ink and the railroader. Properly tempted, Spike made it unanimous.

"About six T-bone steaks, four dozen eggs and enough pie to break our backs might come in pretty handy, too. That flock of coffee we had at daylight didn't mean more than a million dollars' worth of health and strength. How about it?"

"Let's go! I haven't had a full meal with time to eat it for a month," the railroader agreed with justifiable enthusiasm.

"You and me all six," Jimmy the Ink added. "I need a grub lining mighty bad, but first of all I aim to buy you two birds a flock of beer. Lord gosh, it's hot out here in the sun! Mighty glad we don't have to wrassle them long sticks. Look at them thumb-handed loggers jugglin' that stuff."

"Enough men around that timber to eat it," Spike returned, looking over his shoulder toward the quartermaster crew's attack on the timber train as he walked rapidly toward a triangular emporium over which a sign reading: "WINES, LIQUORS AND CIGARS" held forth its promise.

"Three beers."

"Yes, sir." One of the gentlemanly bartenders began to do his stuff.

"And three more coming up," Jimmy echoed, reaching for his first one.

"With three on the bench," chimed the railroader.

With his head tilted back, out of the corners of his eyes when he opened them after the last gulp, standing behind a half-open door which led through a short passageway to the side entrance of the triangular saloon, Jimmy saw a man dressed in an army uniform. Behind this soldier the observer saw a group of figures similarly clad.

He turned for a more direct look before he reached for his second schooner of beer. It seemed to him that the first soldier had beckoned to him.

After he drank the second glass of beer he set it down on the bar and, curious to ascertain the reason for the soldier's summons, he walked slowly toward the half-open door. "Keep drinkin'," he said to Spike. "I'll be back in a second."

He walked through the door and confronted four soldiers. One of them spoke to him in a thirsty whisper. "Listen, pardner —get us some bottles of beer, will you? They won't let us in there with these uniforms on." The whispering soldier shoved a five-dollar bill toward Jimmy.

"And we're dyin' of thirst," another member of the military group added. "It'll be all right if a civilian buys it."

Enjoying to the fullest his personal reactions to the gratifying liquid which he had just consumed, with a characteristic bit of

Fall In! 17

quick friendliness Jimmy shoved back the proffered bank note.

"Keep the change. Stick here. I'll see what I can do."

Returning to the bar where another waiting schooner, capped with its creamy foam, had grounded on the bar, Jimmy salvaged his prize; and then, to the bartender, "Wrap me up a dozen bottles of Bud," he directed. "Get 'em right off the ice, because I got to take 'em clear over to the railroad yards. Gimme an opener along with 'em."

To Spike's questioning glance, preceding the anticipated reminder of the impending T-bone steaks, "Stand hitched," Jimmy whispered. "They're not for us. There's some soldier guys in that side hall who's dyin' of thirst."

When the bottled beer was corraled into a newspaper, roped and tied with a thin white string, and after the trio had poured a fourth cooling set of drinks down their grateful throats, Jimmy, leading his two companions, sauntered over toward the side exit of the saloon. Facing the military quartet, "Park your cash," he said to the first man who held out a handful of silver. "This is on me. Hurry up. Drink hearty. There's three bottles apiece for you—and good luck."

"Here's luck!"

The first four bottles were emptied by the military quartet in record time. Not a man came up for breath until his bottle had been drained.

"Whuf!"

Waiting and ready for the thirsty group, the caps had been removed from four more bottles. One of the soldiers, in his eagerness for the encore, set his empty bottle down on the concrete with a clink.

"Easy, easy! you advertisin' idiot!" one of his companions remonstrated—but the warning was too late.

Through the open door of the saloon came a gentlemanly bartender, spouting legal terms, abstracts from the statutes of New York, quotations from the Constitution of the United States and personal promises of what he intended to do with his trusty beer mallet to violators of the troublesome law relative to selling alcoholic drinks to the defenders of Democracy.

Behind the leader of the charge, eager for contact with the enemy, marched reserves of white-aproned shock troops, and it seemed to the surprised group in the hall that the attacking forces were whining a battle cry whose tenor proclaimed more personal ambition than love of the country's laws.

"Lave me at thim damn sojers!"

"Jese, but they're gittin' brassy wit' their gall—drinkin' ferninst th' very nose of us. Wham! Take that, me fine sojer boy!"

A beer bottle is not a bad weapon in a pinch, and what could be more appropriate for the launching of a bartender out of the back door of his saloon into the front gate of the Hereafter than a beer bottle filled with beer? Bam! Squarely over the fat head of the advance guard of the marching enemy, one of the soldiers busted his libation to Mars.

For only a fraction of a second was this gladiator permitted to contemplate his victory, for, echoing the tinkling glass, came the dull smack of a beer mallet, and he crumpled like a column of custard.

It was at this instant that Spike's resentment of the procedure took the form of action.

"Into it, old rail!" he barked at the railroader. "Hit 'em hard, Jimmy!" he called to his second companion.

Wham! A couple of crunches and a dull thud. Lumberjack stuff! Oh, for calked boots. Well—even with heavy walking shoes a battler trained in the big timber can do a fair piece of felling.

Eleven seconds, and then all the battlefield needed was a thorough renovating.

"Pick up that soldier boy and let's go!" Spike panted. The railroader reached down for the groggy lad in O. D. and, with Spike's assistance, the pair of them got the dazed soldier to his feet. Behind them on the floor, undamaged through the scrap, sat an ice-cold bottle of beer. Jimmy the Ink reached for this bottle. He broke the neck of it off with a quick blow against the concrete floor and before the cold liquid had foamed he dashed it over the head of the semiconscious soldier.

Swimming gestures. "Whuf! Where am I?"

"Get your feet going, kid, and come along."

On the sidewalks of New York, master of all he surveyed, but at the moment lost in a reverie concerning pay day, stood a policeman. "What's this, what's this?" he asked, seeing the seven men.

Spike tried an old one and it worked. "We caught the son-of-a-gun!" he exulted. "Tryin' to desert from the army. When the general gets through with him it'll mean twenty years." Then, starting away from the menace of the law at a quickened pace, "Come along here!" he said to the drooping soldier. "I bet the general hangs you for this."

Clear of their peril, still convoyed by the able-bodied military veterans of the conflict, Spike put an end to a sudden verbal burst of admiration. "That's New York," he said. "That gang of dumb-bells inside the saloon haven't got it figured out yet. Let's get in the clear before that mess of bartenders agree on their story . . . what outfit are you men with?"

"We belong to the Engineers on the boat down there at the long pier. We ducked past the guards and come up here for a scupper of beer and——"

"And here you are—in hell with your back broke," the railroader finished, laboring mightily under the burden of the disabled soldier. "One of you lads take a hand with this heavyweight before my pants fall off."

Various members of the party, observing the railroad man, noted now for the first time that most of his outer raiment was in shreds.

"They kept a-reachin' for me and me tearin' away and soakin' 'em in the guts," he explained, seeking the while to assemble his disordered costume. "I like to tore myself ragged."

Spike laughed, and in his laughter was a note of gratitude. "Good old Rags," he said. "You sure had seven wildcats beat for action. I never saw anybody get himself shredded up so quick before in my life. You look like somebody had snaked you through forty miles of cactus and fed you into a hay baler."

"Gimme a belt or somethin' or a pair of suspenders so I can cinch these pants a little closer on me," the railroader returned.

"Hell, Rags, you don't need no belt! What you need is a clothing store, includin' socks and shirts and how are you fixed for neckties? Keep going, Rags, you fightin' fool, till we get this soldier back to his gang—and then we start out for a joint where you can get dressed up before the purity squad pinches you."

Nearing the pier the disabled soldier had recovered sufficiently to walk alone. "We'll leave you fellows here," Spike said to the soldier crew. "You don't need our help gettin' through the lines?"

"Gettin' back is a cinch. Gettin' out past those sentries was the big job," one of the Engineers replied. "And listen to me, old-timer," he continued, holding out his hand, "you birds sure made four friends for yourself back there!"

"Forget it. Give your bayonet an extry twist for me when you shove it through the

Kaiser's guts, and we'll call it square . . . I might see you over there some day. So long and good luck."

With Jimmy and the newly christened Rags, Spike made his way to the tracks where the timber train had been spotted. "Maybe that brass-bound fathead will sign Uncle Sam's name on the receipts for that timber now that he's getting it on the ship," Spike offered when the trio got to where they could survey the laboring crew which thronged between the empty flat cars and the *Starvonia*.

In reply Jimmy the Ink, galvanized by something he saw ahead of him, halted abruptly and squinted his eyes for a keener glance at the drama of destruction which lay suddenly revealed.

"By the bellerin' Babe ox of the holy rollin' Paul Bunyan!" he yelled. "Look at them crosscut saws! Look what them dumb damned soldiers have done to our ninety-foot sticks!"

Spike trotted three paces to the front and then, shutting his eyes, he shook his head and whined like an eager wolf. Boiling slugs of rich sulphuric vocabulary vibrated from his lips like live steam from a superheated boiler at the instant of its explosion.

The cause of Spike's anguish was evident even to the railroader,— "They're cuttin' 'em up!"

"Nursin' them ninety-foot sticks three thousand miles across the country, only to have 'em sawed up into short stuff by the army!" Spike had resumed his trot. In three strides he shifted into a gallop, but when he got nearly to the sweating crews about the unloaded timber his gallop slowed to a walk and in his attitude, the droop of his shoulders, could be read discouragement and a surrender to hopeless odds.

Of the ninety-foot stuff, cut now into short sections, not a stick remained intact.

"Where's the boss quartermaster?" In a dull voice Spike questioned an idle soldier.

"Down there by the boat," the soldier answered.

Facing the quartermaster colonel, Spike exploded one question in that officer's face.

"What the hell's the big idea of choppin' this stuff up into kindling?"

Thereafter for a space of ninety seconds, laboring mightily to control a fatal impulse to bust the colonel in the nose, Spike had the big idea outlined to him along with a gratuitous oration relative to military dignity, the insignificance of civilians, outraged pomposity and Who was Who in the army.

Then, regaining a frazzled fragment of his justly celebrated military dignity, the popping fat colonel condescended to impart a wheeze relative to the Habit of Obedience. "I have orders to load this timber on the *Starvonia,* sir! It cannot be stowed in ninety-foot lengths, and therefore I have cut it up into thirty-foot sections. I will sign your receipts for this timber, sir, and that will end our official relationship."

Mastering himself with no small difficulty, but sensing the wisest course, Spike kept his mouth shut and reached for the crumpled documents which were buttoned in a pocket inside his vest. When the quartermaster colonel's signature, which meant cash compensation to King Timber, Inc., had been affixed to the receipts, not trusting himself in further contact with the officer, Spike spoke quickly to his two companions. "Come along with me."

Indulging their criticism of the event, Jimmy and Rags followed Spike at a rapid pace back to the caboose wherein the trio had traveled from Chicago to New York. In the caboose, Spike folded the signed receipts for the mutilated timber and put them in an envelope bearing the printed address of the Seattle office of King Timber, Inc.

He handed the sealed envelope to Jimmy the Ink.

"Shove that in a mail box, Jimmy, and when you see the Old Man in Seattle tell him I went on ahead. If that colonel bird is a sample of the regular army talent it's a cinch the hundred million folks at home will need some ordinary average human beings to play their game in France . . . So long, kid,"— Spike held out his hand to Jimmy the Ink— "Keep 'em rollin', Rags,"—he laid his hand on the railroader's shoulder— "That Engineer Outfit don't know it yet, but they've hired a new hand!"

Jimmy the Ink, reverting to a poker phrase that had cost him something less than a million dollars, burst out with a declaration of his personal program.

"Wild man, I see that and raise you one. Spike, them Engineers have hired two hands!"

Rags the railroader, following a calm and contemplative four seconds, stood for the raise and did his bit before the draw. "Three and out!" he exclaimed. "I'm riding with you two sawbucks for the run. The military stuff has got railroadin' ruined, anyhow—and besides that I'll save me the price of a suit of clothes by gettin' into a uniform."

"Let's go!"

Within the hour, the last three men to join the Regiment before it sailed, Spike and Jimmy and Rags, clearing the medicos, had signed on with the Engineers and had taken the oath that made them a part of the advance ripple of the first wave of volunteers that sailed to France.

Fall In! 29

The *Starvonia* cleared at eight o'clock that night.

Eight o'clock and all was well with the Regiment—save that one Corporal Badger, the adjutant's dog and the Demon Rum were strolling blithely hand in hand somewhere in New York when the ship sailed—and that the medicos, beginning a record of error, diagnosed a first-class case of smallpox as the measles—and that a member of the guard, studying his newly acquired .45, splashed a bullet through the deck above him and wondered, pop-eyed, how it happened—and that less than twelve per cent of the Regiment answered the first false alarm which summoned them to the boats—and that no ammunition had been taken aboard for the two antisub guns with which the *Starvonia* was equipped; and that eighty per cent of the rations for the Regiment had been left on the dock—and that the ship suddenly appeared to be infested with mascots and military mannerisms.

Colonel Ross, listening to his adjutant's report, smiled to the bitter end of that West Pointer's snappy recital, and then with true philosophic calm he poured himself a slug of likker three sizes larger than his usual nightcap and started on a prowl through the ship.

Included in the enlisted personnel of the Regiment were a hundred old-timers who had worked along the West Coast on various jobs with Spike and Jimmy the Ink, but so far Spike had encountered none of his former construction mates.

Leaning against the ship's rail while she steamed down the calm waters of the harbor, Spike's mood changed with each passing minute. Once, remembering the great organization which he had served so well, he questioned the wisdom of his course.

Then, set against this, he saw as well as one man could a brief flash of the great enterprise of destruction which lay ahead.

Well, intelligently, in return for what the dear great land had meant to him, he would give all of his brain, all of his strength, all of his power, his force, his skill, gladly and freely, playing the game to the finish, whatever that finish might be. . . . "Private

Fall In! 31

Spike Randall" . . . He smiled in the darkness, thinking of the extensive authority over other men which he had enjoyed under the direction of Old Man King. Railroads and camps and mills, projects of King Timber—pioneering half of these enterprises, Spike Randall had blazed the trail, marching through against heavy odds—"because the Old Man leaned on me." Spike reached for a cigarette and lighted it. "He'll be sore as hell at first, then he'll call me a damn fool, then he'll see the point . . ."

Abruptly out of the darkness: "Douse that cigarette! You're under arrest. Come with me."

Three decks down, in a little area roped off against a bulkhead and guarded by a dozen superfluous soldiers, was the first "guardhouse" that Spike had ever seen.

Spike looked at his watch. "Not so bad. Hour and forty minutes—and pinched."

When the formalities of incarceration had been accomplished, Spike smiled at a group of his fellow prisoners. "What are you in for?" he asked the nearest man.

"Spittin' on deck, jailbird. Why did they soak you?"

"Lighting a cigarette."

It appeared that Victim Number Three had failed to salute an officer. "He wasn't one of the Gang, though. He was our regimental adjutant that come from West Point. He's a regular nut on salutes."

Number Four had been detected in the act of looking at the luminous dial of his new wrist watch on the open deck where peeking periscopes might observe his deed.

Felony and high crime—but the discomforts of the guardhouse were none the less real.

At nine o'clock, prowling along under the dim light of the shaded electric bulbs, came the colonel of the Regiment. Sighting the culprits, the countenance of Colonel Ross assumed a mask of severity, but deep in the Colonel's kindly eyes there twinkled a kindling light. "A good man to have for your friend when the real trouble comes along," Spike reflected.

Ten minutes after the Colonel had disappeared, a brisk young officer wearing the single silver bars on his shoulders came pacing along on the regimental commander's trail.

"Where'd the Colonel go?" he asked one of the guards.

In an effort to remember all of the complex ritual concerning relationship between officer and enlisted man, the guard began to perform tricks on the rifle. Before the calisthenics got violent, "Nix on that sign language, old man—which way did the Colonel go?"

"Down that way, Lootenant." The guard held his rifle with one hand and pointed in a nonmilitary manner with the other.

"What are these men doing in here?" the lieutenant asked.

"They're in jail, sir," answered two other guards simultaneously. "This is the guardhouse."

"What are they guilty of, I mean? I'm Officer of the Day, to-night—that's the reason I'm interested."

Beginning the chorus of confession, the

spitter explained his case in two words: "I spit."

At the end of the inventory of crime, "I lit a cigarette," Spike admitted.

The Lieutenant smiled and then, half to himself, he indulged in what might have developed into a hearty laugh except that it was terminated at its inception by the quick words of a general pardon. "What the hell! Not guilty—report to your company officers for company discipline. All out! Tell the sergeant of the guard to let me sign the book. Play the game next time, and keep out of trouble. You're in the army now."

When the pardon-bearing officer had resumed his pursuit of the Colonel, "That's a B Company Loot," one of the transgressors announced. "He used to be a railroader but he's in the bridge game now."

"He's in the army now, you mean, just like you and me. Remember what he said, if you want to duck the grief."

Ducking the grief is a grand thing in theory but mighty difficult in practice. Recounting his experience to Jimmy the Ink and Rags,

Spike wound up his story with a warning to the young. "Play the game," he advised. "It's the only way you can side-step the military mess. You're in the army now."

Up ahead, not so very far, great gobs of grief lay waiting—rich, luscious disaster to be suffered or side-stepped in a military manner by Spike and his shipmates, depending on the way the cards might drop from the stacked deck of Lady Luck.

Chapter 2

HEAVE HO!

DAWN and the deep blue sea. The rolling *Starvonia* lurched into a green groove of the Atlantic and a struggling bugler abandoned his solo and devoted himself to a convulsive attempt to turn himself inside out.

Half awake and feeling middling rotten, Jimmy the Ink came back to reality with the first notes of the bugle. He lifted somebody's feet off his neck and sat up in the narrow bunk. All about him men were groaning salutations to the dawn, but he focused his attention on the advertising bugler.

"Whuf! Lemme out of here!" Jimmy began a forced march to a stairway which led to air and daylight.

He was followed by all of the able-bodied members of the crew about him.

"Choke that belching bugler bird to death!" somebody called, but by this time the disabled bugler, striving to eradicate a form-fitting attack of seasickness, was choking himself to death in a manner calculated to satisfy the most insistent advocates of violence. There is a gratifying command, "Fire at will," and before Jimmy the Ink had gained the stairway of escape the men behind him were obeying that command.

On deck, the cool morning air served to revive some of the outfit, but it seemed as if the physical distress of the convalescents had been transferred to the less fortunate victims of the shuddering *Starvonia*.

Spike Randall, as yet able-bodied but facing a poisonous green future, draped Rags and Jimmy the Ink over the ship's rail, which was already thickly festooned with casualties. Then, before example and suggestion could begin their work, he turned to seek some happier sight, but all about him lay grief in assorted sizes.

A group of officers, headed by the Colonel of the Regiment, came clicking down the deck, and with some satisfaction Spike noted that their military manner was all gummed up.

A medico, explaining something to the Colonel, used a gangrenous technical term, and the Colonel, falling out, retired precipitately to the rail.

The Colonel having set the example, to say nothing of a mark to shoot at, he was followed by six or seven assorted gentlemen in whom the President of the United States, over his signature, had reposed special confidence.

Well, roughly translated the word "Essayons" embossed on the brass buttons adorning the Engineer officer's uniform means "Keep Striving." This they did, led by a corpulent major who put on a fair imitation of Old Faithful after that geyser had been annoyed with a cake of soap administered internally.

When some of the gushers had gone to gas, in the parlance of the oil fields, and when others had sanded up, into the picture, wearing spurs, came the regimental adjutant. He clicked his heels in the approved manner and came to attention smartly on the port side of the gasping commander of the Regiment.

Saluting with a most disgusting perfection, "Does the Colonel wish to proceed with the inspection?" he inquired.

Spike Randall listened attentively for the Colonel's reply, hoping for the best. In this he was not disappointed. Rising figuratively from his bed of pain, the Colonel justified his listeners' fondest hopes in a last will and testament rendered in a sulphuric tremolo which affected the perfect adjutant about as an ounce of salt affects a snail.

The adjutant dissolved into his boots; and his boots, with their spurs tinkling merrily, walked away with their wilted cargo.

"Lord gosh, that Colonel of ours is sure human," Rags gasped at Spike from where he hung with one arm over the ship's rail.

"Human! Say, boy—help me remember that last burst of language. That was the most ornate bunch of speech that's been put out since Paul Bunyan tried to stick the brandin' iron on the Babe Ox."

"This all started when them doctors taught

us to turn our stummicks inside out and say 'ah,'" a groaning soldier observed.

"I'll tell the cockeyed world we don't need nobody to tell us what the next word after 'ah' is," a feeble listener observed, and then, into a comparative calm came another covey of bugle notes interspaced with gargling misfires.

"Breakfast! Come and get it."

"Don't crave me no breakfast. Don't even say that breakfast word to me!" The speaker gagged and returned disgustedly to his morning's work.

Spike Randall, needing his morning coffee, began the long descent to where Breakfast at Sea was being served. Three decks down, in a wide compartment reeking with complex odors, two or three hundred good sailors of the Regiment had gathered. Gentlemanly guides, clinging to stanchions, half of them with their eyes tightly shut against the scene before them, were bawling directions to the breakfast seekers. "B Company this way!" A hearty hiccup.

Following directions, Spike and thirty or

forty members of Company B rallied at two long tables whereon, slithering about in a ghastly gravy, a half-submerged mass of cows' livers provided a background for clicking conoids of hard-boiled hen eggs, some of which, freshly out of their tortures in the steam kettles, popped viciously at their hesitating attackers.

"Liver! Holy jo-heeveley! And me gagged already. Lemme out! Good-by, Lootenant——"

The victim of his own imagination sped past one of the company officers who had been detailed to escort his men through the perils of breakfast.

"Urrgh-ik! Look at the purple edge on that liver—lemme out of here!"

"That damned quivering liver looks like a cable car accident I seen once."

Pssst-tk! An egg with a slow fuse began to unfold a panorama of all that an egg should not be, bang in the faces of three physical culture enthusiasts who at once forgot their begun breakfast ambitions and sought the open air.

"Java! Where at is the coffee? Come a-runnin' with that Jamokus juice!"

" 'Arf a mo'!" One of the ship's galley crew, sloshing about in the moving mosaic of the floor, smirked and displayed a full set of brown and busted teeth. He ducked away and returned to one of the B Company tables a moment later, bearing an immense coffee-pot.

" 'Ere you are, steamin' 'ot." Into a dozen waiting cups splashed a lukewarm liquid.

Spike tasted the decoction. Tea! A tea of boots and chicken feathers, of tanbark and garlic. "Whuf!"

Another victim of the coffee habit swallowed a mouthful of the liquid, and when his facial contortions had quieted, to the galley man, "Where do you come from that you call this coffee?" he asked.

"I comes from Liverpool, sir—" the steward began, and then, before he could explain why, he retreated in the face of an impromptu riot whose principal manifestation was a shower of liver. "Here's your liverpool!"

The second volley was explosive eggs.

The third volley, delivered quietly, ended the riot. It consisted of a few sympathetic words from the Loot, along with a cast-iron admonition in which the Gang discovered some quality that meant business. "Can the rough stuff, you birds," the Loot advised. "One more outburst of joy and gladness and there'll be another mess of agitated livers hit the ceiling. Live through it, Gang. Get that tea down your neck some way. It'll do you good."

Experimenting with the eggs, Spike managed to find a comparatively modern trio. "Load 'em heavy with pepper and you can eat 'em," he advised the man to his left. "Fish out some with the yellow shells and——"

The advice was interrupted by another bugle call, and a perfectly appointed medico drifted into view. He looked about him with a cold, dispassionate eye. "Filthy," he remarked, and then, turning to the regimental adjutant, who accompanied him: "It might be a good plan to have men detailed from each company to clean up this mess after each meal, Captain," he suggested. "Look at the bread on the floor there, and the gravy spilled over everything. Look at those fragments of liver sloshing about. See those stewpans spilling over their contents on the table—and the eggshells everywhere—those broken eggs on the floor——"

Evidently hypnotized, but still capable of independent action, the adjutant brought his right hand up in the first theatrical gesture of a salute, but he stopped the hand with his finger tips tightly pressed over his twitching mouth. The adjutant, obeying the medico's suggestion, had let his attention drift over various points of interest until, coming to an especially luscious segment of liver, he surrendered to some influence stronger than his military training and, with his new spurs twinkling through the steamy vapors of the banquet hall, he trotted up the stairway to where the bright blue sky might form a canopy over whatever earthly remains should be left after an oversized set of seasickness had been subtracted from what had once been an Officer and a Gentleman, half and half.

"The captains and the kings depart," Spike Randall reflected, returning to his third and last egg.

Darkness before dawn. By noon on their first day out, Jimmy and Rags had recovered from their seasickness, and the Regiment as a whole included less than fifty victims of the malady. Good men they were, and rapidly they became good sailors.

True enough, Corporal Badger was missing with the adjutant's dog, and the man with the smallpox seemed to be stubborn about having his measles cured, but a general inspection early in the afternoon justified the Colonel's faith in the Regiment.

Prowling around and getting acquainted, Spike and Jimmy and Rags encountered numerous old-timers whom they had known in the construction world. They found Slim and Shorty and Chuck, Red Walker and Old Pop Sibley, Riff Swenson, Blackie, Jugger, Isadog and Mike and the singing trio from Skikomish—Tex, Rex and Mex.

Recurrent reunions marked the hour, and it was filled with news of companions who had drifted here and there across the West, following up the various industries and enterprises of that wide domain.

Out of the mass the Rabble formed, and the Rabble crew were all old-timers.

Forming a second subdivision came the Gang, and almost before the sun had set on their first day at sea the Gang, numbering twenty-five or thirty members, had formed about some undefined nucleus of mutual interests and friendships which, through the long months to come, were to bind them into one of the most exclusive organizations of wild men in the A. E. F.

Following two or three sub scares—England.

An hour before the *Starvonia* landed, the Loot sought Spike Randall. "Cap has made you a sergeant," the Loot announced. "I'm glad of it."

He held out his hand to Spike, and then and there an unwritten compact which was to endure through all the stresses of the coming months was signed, sealed and delivered.

"What does a sergeant have to do, Loot?" Spike inquired. "I've had mighty little chance to size things up, and this army game is all new stuff to me."

"Your main job is to get hard when you have to—and to bear down heavy now and then. You've got to be blind and deaf and dumb the rest of the time," the Loot returned. "The army stuff is as new to me as it is to you—don't let it worry you. As a matter of fact, to hell with it. We hired on as workin' stiffs, didn't we?"

"I get you. Fair enough."

"Forty ways! Keep your eye on the wild men for a while after we land. In spite of all their care-free girlish laughter, the outfit is still a little bit keyed up about that last sub. They're mighty apt to take on an overdose of likker if they get a chance. Watch the cut when we land. Nothing teetotal, Spike, but don't let 'em overplay the hooch hand."

In contrast with the glittering brass, the polished leather, the serge and the whipcord which adorned their hosts of the hour, the Regiment's sartorial equipment looked like something from the top shelf, but the Britishers were good guessers and nothing was lacking in the warmth of the greeting which they gave the new arrivals.

A Scotch band played the Engineers off the *Starvonia* and thrilled them with the wild music of the pipes while hot blood surged with each recurrent bamming of the battering drums.

"These birds are good guys," the Regiment decided, and this first judgment found confirmation in every event of their later associations.

In the long pier shed where the outfit rested pending some act of Parliament which would afford them a bath some two weeks overdue, a new flock of regimental orders was promulgated to while away the time. Along came an orderly dealing out unreasonable demands. He faced the Loot, who had stuck with the company while his various brother officers had gone uptown to see about something or other. The Loot signed for the tissue copies of half a dozen orders. He looked at the messenger.

"You better steady those hind legs, boy," he advised. "Keep walking before you fall down."

"Lieutenant, I didn't have but one drink."

"You must have breathed mighty deep before you took it. On your way before it begins steaming."

The Loot glanced down at the top order: "To be read to all men of the company: Indulgence in alcoholic beverages is absolutely forbidden during——"

The Loot called Spike Randall over to him and handed him the order. "First issue of the comic supplement on foreign shores," he said. "Bear it in mind and do the best you can with the outfit."

The second order covered gambling. The third, inspired by one of the regimental surgeons, sought to erect a protective bulwark between Mars and Venus. "Ever striving for the good, the true, the beautiful," the Loot reflected, and then his attention was suddenly drawn to the unwarranted popularity of three or four members of a water detail about whose brimming buckets the Gang had clustered with some unusual alacrity.

He sauntered over to one of these groups.

" 'Tenshun, men!" A military member of the Gang, laden with a clouded conscience, spoke a warning to his fellows.

"Lend me that cup when you finish," the Loot asked one of the Gang. He took the cup and dipped deeply into one of the water buckets. He lifted the cup to his lips and it was brimming full of rich dark beer, cold and clear. The Loot drank and returned the cup to its owner. "Whuf! The water in England has a mighty grand taste to it," he remarked, so that half the Gang might hear him.

Quick smiles, bespeaking the end of sudden doubts, followed the Loot's comment. "Hit 'er again, Loot. We got a artesian well of it back of the barn."

The Loot shook his head and smiled. "Don't let the sheep-herders poison your well," he advised, walking away.

Thereafter the odds were better than ten to

one against any member of the Gang who sought to absorb an overload of alcohol. "Play the game," the majority advised, seeing to it that the thirst-bearer played the game.

"The temperate habits of your men are most remarkable," a British officer observed to the Colonel of the Regiment some time later.

Before the Colonel could voice his formal acceptance of the compliment, "I'm glad you observed that, sir," the regimental adjutant returned. "It speaks well for the ready acceptance of the discipline we imposed by a regimental order forbidding indulgence in alcoholic drinks."

"Oh, God," groaned the British officer to himself, and then aloud, pleasantly, "Oh, rully! I say—rully!"

From the distant barracks wherein, for the night, the Gang was quartered, came the echoes of a slightly discordant chorus. "One keg of beer for the four of us!"

The Rest Camp.

"Hell, them ain't bedbugs. Get away

from one, boy—don't you know personal insects when you see 'em? Them's cooties."

"I never saw any before."

"Git a lookin'-glass and ramble over your own geography and you'll see plenty. They never come single. That's a mighty queer thing about cooties."

"Naw, sir," another comforter explained, "they travel in tribes just like Indians."

"What do you do for 'em?" Itching now over half of his anatomy, the embryo naturalist wriggled here and there underneath his heavy issue underwear.

"They respond quick to gentle treatment. Three meals a day, bed the herd down at night and you'd be surprised how they flourish. They're mighty easy to raise."

"Hell—I don't want to raise none! I mean, what do you do to get rid of 'em?"

"That's different. About the only thing you can do is to hunt up somebody that's equipped with another tribe that's enemies to the ones you got. Like I knew a man once on the Columbia River canal job that raised himself a tribe of Flathead cooties. They was gentle enough and slept quiet all night, but after a while they got to holdin' family reunions and you'd be surprised how many relatives come to the gatherin's.

"Finally the fella got tired of it. He cussed a lot and used force and everything but did they leave him? Naw, sir. There was the grandfather and the grandmother, thirty-eight families and half a pint of uncles and aunts and children enough runnin' around at them family reunions to keep half a dozen men from gettin' lonely. Couldn't get rid of 'em any more than he could outrun his shadow on a moonlight night.

"Finally asked me what to do. 'Hunt up a savage tribe that are enemies to yours,' I told him, so he prowled around until he run into a fella from Canada that had a lot of them Saskatchewan cooties, and, boy, you ought to see them two tribes go to it! When the battle ended they wasn't a cootie left except one old Flathead grandfather, and them two owners laid him on a anvil and took a sledge hammer and hit him a crack and there they was, lonesome as could be and with no more company in their shirts than a fish has feathers——"

"Ain't there any easier way of gettin' rid of 'em?" the cootie owner asked, writhing with increased enthusiasm.

Answering the question with another question, "Boy, how many years of age are you?" the older man inquired.

"I'm a little over twenty-one—you can see it on my service papers."

"If you've turned eighteen I'm old Methusalum. Trouble is, you're too green to burn, or I'd advise you to start a forest fire along in the underbrush and when them cooties come out in the open you could pop 'em off with a sling shot. Failin' that, about all I know of is soap and water and a good hot bath. The soap gets in their eyes and the water makes 'em think there's a flood and they start runnin' for high ground and tromple each other to death, account they can't see good. You better hurry up and try it."

The cootie bearer left in search of the hot bath, but long before he had attained his object a bugle halted him and he noticed that the Regiment had awakened to a new activity. Assembly blew, and when the companies had formed word came down the line that the Regiment was to move.

"Hell, I thought they said this was a rest camp where we was goin' to stay five days!"

"You're so far north that the days is only an hour long. . . . Lemme help you empty that old bottle. There's mighty likely to be a damn inspection."

Within the hour the Regiment had resumed its journey, and, late that night, packed tightly into a ship which had been used as a horse transport, it saw the chalk cliffs of England, white in the moonlight, fade astern and France lie up ahead.

At dawn, off the jetty at Le Havre, a frazzled soldier poked his head up over a hatch coaming, only to encounter an agitated sentry.

"Halt!" barked the sentry who had been prompted to assume his discarded military manner by a glimpse of the land where the Big Game was being played.

Heave Ho!   57

"Where do you get that 'Halt' stuff? Say 'Whoa!' to me when you want me to stop. Boy,—I'm a horse! Smell me and see if I ain't."

"Gee-haw, brother—back to your stall before I unhitch you from the army."

The horse backed into his stall according to orders, but he emerged presently along with his companions to enjoy his first view of Sunny France, which was just then lying soggy under a delayed cloudburst.

The Regiment went ashore in the rain. "We get breakfast up ahead at a British rest camp," somebody announced.

"Boy, I'm mighty shy of these rest camps."

"I'm mighty shy of breakfast. I don't care when it happens."

Breakfast consisted of tea and boiled potatoes, with a side order of bread. "Bread if you can call it bread. More like rubber. Bite it off square or it'll fly back at you."

At ten o'clock the regimental surgeons made a third and last inspection of the smallpox patient. "All you had was prickly heat," the regimental surgeon announced.

"That first doctor said I had measles."

"He was mistaken. So was the second one, who told you you had smallpox."

The prickly heat patient joined his company in time to stand at attention for an hour and a half preparing for a regimental muster.

After the first thirty minutes of this endurance contest, Rags the railroader whispered to the sergeant behind him:

"Holy crust, Spike, how long is this gonna last?"

"I'm damned if I know."

An hour more, and word came down the line that the field desks containing the regimental records, together with all of the company records, had been left in England due to an oversight on the part of the regimental adjutant.

"Dis-missed!"

"Three cheers for the adjutant!"

The Assembly. "Fall in with packs." There came a four-mile march, and then another rumor relative to a rest camp which presently materialized. The packs were unslung. "We got three days here instead of them three days we missed over in England."

"Roll in, big boy. Hit the hay!"

"You're doggone right I will. Didn't get me no sleep a-tall last night."

Here it was that the youthful cootie pioneer found lots of misery to keep him company. It seemed as if the parasite world had made of this place a concentration camp. "All the bugs in the world are right here in this little old corner of France."

"Shut up. Get to sleep. For the love of tripe, what's a few indoor grasshoppers? G'wan to sleep and forget it."

Thirty-five minutes after the Gang got settled a bugle call promoted by the regimental surgeons awakened one man out of every thirty. "Roll out, you birds! Come a-runnin'!" It appeared that one of the medicos had discovered that the last shot in the arm, instead of being the third of the typhoid series, was a hay fever serum. The awakened Gang, yawning and grumbling, stumbled down the line to where the needle workers did their stuff, but neither the constant rain nor sore arms nor interrupted sleep nor prospecting parasites could offset the cheering gossip concerning the hearty meal which was being prepared.

"Boy, there's a hundred cooks around them kitchens. Big joints of beef and all the jam in the world and I must of seen a thousand pies."

"Say, old-timer, I can use it. Sure relish some rations! I ain't had me no nutriment or nuthin' else since that tea and potatoes we had for breakfast."

Systematic prowling revealed a basis of truth underlying the rumor concerning the luscious qualities of the forthcoming supper. A little apart from the rest camp, busy about sizzling field stoves, sure enough there were forty or fifty cooks.

"How come them boys is English cooks? What are our cooks doin'?"

"Helpin' lug in the wines, likkers and cigars for our big banquet, probably. The way my stummick feels it'd take all the cooks we got and a lot of help from the British to round up enough grub to fill it. Wonder what's delayin' that Mess Call? Look at that roast beef! If I ever saw anything done to a turn, that beef is!"

The speaker was distracted from the roast beef by the arrival of a missing member of the Gang.

"Old Corporal Badger! Well, I'm a son-of-a-gun!"

"I be damned if the old prodigal son himself isn't back!"

"Where'd you come from, you army deserter?"

When appropriate greetings had been exchanged, "I got detailed to take the adjutant's dog out for a walk in civilian clothes there in New York, so the first thing I know that dog led me on board a ferryboat and kept a-pullin' on his string after we landed and the next thing I saw was Broadway loomin' up right in my face. That dog led me up and down Broadway, in and out of more saloons than you could count on a cash register.

"You never saw a dog talk as plain as he did. 'It's about time we was gettin' back to the boat,' I said to him along around three o'clock. 'Never mind the boat,' he spoke back. 'Take me into a couple of more good saloons where they have that nice cold beer. I like to see you drink it.'

"So I took him into a couple of more saloons or so, and the next thing I know I meet a fella I was on a steam-shovel job with when we was double-trackin' the S. P. He was damn near as bad as the dog—kept leadin' me in and out of saloons till my head got numb. Soon as that numb feelin' kind of left me, I looked at the calendar and I be a son-of-a-gun if four days hadn't drifted by! Well, I figgered the army couldn't move no faster than a single unmarried man, and so I caught me a steamboat for France, trailin' you boys up."

"How'd you know where we was, with nobody allowed to put nothing in his letters by the censors?"

"Censors didn't say anything about newspapers, did they? All I did was read the papers till I saw where the Regiment had landed in England and was gonna sail for the French town of Larvey in a couple of days."

"What become of the adjutant's pooch—you bring him with you all the way?"

"Boy, the last thing that dog said to me when I met Jim Crane there on Broadway was, 'Go along into war-torn France if you got to. Little old Broadway is good enough for me.' Last I see of him he was headed for Fifth Avenue. He seemed to be a mighty high-toned dog in some ways. Chances is he went into a rest camp up in Central Park where they is lots of trees."

"You tell the adjutant about that dog yet?"

"What do the army regulations say about trivial conversation between enlisted men and ossifers?—not me. That adjutant's got enough to take care of, losing regiment records according to what I hear and everything, without being pestered by a ordinary corporal . . . How they been feedin' you boys?"

"They been feedin' us——"

A bugle interrupted the speaker. "There's the chow call. Come along and we'll show you how grand they feeds us in this man's army. Roast beef and pie and—doggone it, that ain't no Mess Call! That's Assembly! I'm gettin' so I can tell 'em apart."

The companies fell in. Five minutes later a covey of orderlies delivered emergency orders to each company commander, covering the latest phase of one of the minor horrors of war.

"We entrain immediately," the Loot announced after a brief consultation with his superior officer. Then, to Spike: "Grab Rags and Jugger and Fat and two or three more of the Gang and beat it over to that supply depot. We take on an issue of emergency rations to eat on the train. Report to Shorty the cook. He's over there now with Jimmy the Ink, fighting the paper work. Bring the stuff down to the train."

Half an hour later, staggering along under ponderous boxes of borrowed rations, the chow detail passed the field kitchens which, a little while before, had held out their invitations of roast beef, apple pie and assorted delicacies.

"Well, I'll be a second-hand son of a half-soled boot! Who d'ya suppose is eatin' up that banquet—look at them damn German prisoners sinkin' their fangs into them rations!"

"On your way, rebel. You're in the army now."

Presently the rebel and all of the rest of the Regiment were climbing into the dark interior of a long train of cars built to accommodate 8 horses, 40 men.

In the crowded darkness, "Move over, you elephant! You'd think them eight horses was in here with us forty men."

"When do we eat?"

"Kill them cooties before you throw 'em away! And listen, boy, don't throw any more of them cooties this way or I'll bust you in the beak!"

Stumbling along in the dim lantern light beside the train came the chow detail on the final lap of its race. "Take these here boxes. Reach down and grab this stuff. Go easy on it. Bust it open and eat it, whatever the hell it is."

In the darkness, after the first heavy cases

of tinned edibles had been delivered to each carload of voracious victims of "rest camp" régime, there came numerous smaller boxes, and these were not so heavy as the ones which contained the goldfish and the bully beef.

"Handle this mighty easy."

"What you got?"

"Listen, boy—it's vinegar to go onto your alligator pears."

To the Loot, riding for congenial company in the cattle car with Rags and Blackie and the rest of the Gang, Shorty Goodwin, the company cook, delivered one of the cases of vinegar. "Try this vinegar on that salmon, Lieutenant. I got sixty cases of it out of that supply depot. They tell me it's plenty good vinegar."

Something in Shorty's tone impelled the Loot to investigate the vinegar.

The cover of the case came off just as the long train started for Somewhere in France. The Loot lifted out a straw-padded bottle of the "vinegar."

By the light of his lantern he read under the larger type of the label, "Very Old Vatted

Scotch." He turned to Shorty the cook, who stood watching him.

"How many cases of vinegar did you get?"

Smiling faintly at the hard-boiled tone of the Loot's voice, "Sixty cases altogether, Lieutenant—ten for each company."

The cork was out of the Lieutenant's very old bottle of vatted Scotch by this time. In the darkness Shorty heard seven gratifying gurgles coming from somewhere around the Lieutenant's vocal organs, and then, "You must have made a mistake, Shorty," the Loot said. "That isn't vinegar. It tastes more like maple syrup."

"Lieutenant, yes, sir. That's the way that malt vinegar tastes."

The Loot took another crack at the vinegar. "Here's luck! . . . I'm mighty glad you made that mistake, Shorty," he said. "So is everybody else from the way they sound. Listen . . ."

Up and down the train, rising high above the clanking fabric of the cars, sounded various voices raised in song, "One keg of beer for the four of us!"

Hearing these song birds, back in his car the Colonel smiled at his adjutant. "The morale of the Regiment appears to be all that one could desire, Captain," the Colonel observed.

"Yes, indeed, Colonel—there were some welfare workers in camp, distributing chocolate and cigarettes just before we entrained. . . . It takes so little to make our soldier boys happy."

At this the Colonel frowned slightly. "I wonder where the hell I can find a good adjutant," he mused.

At midnight in the long rumbling train, in spite of cooties and hunger, in spite of being wet and dirty and on their way toward the center of life's big question mark the Regiment, the Rabble, the Gang slept peacefully, trusting Lady Luck to carry them through whatever awaited them up ahead.

Chapter 3

Entente Cordiale and Other Drinks

NEARING Paris, the Gang contemplated the delights and perils of that wicked city. Following a rumor that all-day passes would be issued the moment the train stopped in front of the Eiffel Tower there came a sudden demand for a few essential words of the French language.

"How do you tell a girl it is a fine day?" somebody inquired.

"You wait a couple of weeks till the sun shines and then point to it. Where do you get that fine day stuff!"

"What do you say to a French gal when you ask her if she craves to take a stroll along the boulevard?"

"That ain't what worries me—what do you say to her when you get fed up on strolling?"

"Say, boy—don't let that worry you

neither. Just tell 'em 'Ah, oui, Sister' to everything and you're bound to win every bet."

"I aim to duck these madamsells," Jugger announced. "I aim to devote myself to likker. You don't need no language for likker over here. All you say is Vang Blank, Vang Rooge or Coonyak, and when you get so you can't say neither one they keep bringin' it anyhow. . . . Wish I had me another bottle of Shorty's vinegar."

All of these visions of delight gave way to a cold realization of the fact that collectively the Gang was out of luck when the train turned southward from Paris without stopping. All day long and steadily through the second acutely uncomfortable night the Regiment was hauled toward an unknown destination.

In the late afternoon of the second day of the journey, arriving at one of the suburbs of Bordeaux, the train stopped. "All out! You're mighty close to home, sweet home," a trotting orderly from the Colonel's car announced to each carload of 40 hommes.

"Where do we go from here?"

Shorty Goodwin, the company cook, volunteered an answer. "You birds go straight from here to a square meal if I can get a fire going," but there was a delay in the square meal, due to some complicated arrangement whereby, after backing and filling for half an hour, the Regiment straightened out in its march up a long hill to where, according to an optimistic French liaison officer, some of the best barracks in France awaited the welcome newcomers.

"The barracks—of what perfection! It is as the officer commanding this region, General Goizet-Diderot, has said, that nothing is perfect enough for these brave American friends of France."

Well, for one thing the barracks at Genimont were not perfect enough for these friends of France. Shower baths existed—but there was no water for them. The barracks had roofs over them, to be sure, but the roofs leaked. There was straw for a motley assortment of bed sacks, but these sacks swarmed with animal life and the straw was moldy.

"The most modern and elaborate culinary arrangement for the kitchen," the French liaison officer explained, "is contemplated. Alas, at the moment perhaps—what you call it?—the camp fire will suffice."

Hearing this, "Then again perhaps not," the Loot amended, aiming his remark at Spike Randall. "Get a detail and limber up those field kitchens so Shorty can get to work," the Loot directed. "Bust out two or three scouting expeditions and see what we can do for some clean straw. Ball those damn bed sacks up and get 'em outside the huts. Hang onto those lanterns—looks like we might have to play another night shift and there are no lights in the damn camp."

The Regiment dined on goldfish and coffee. Taps at ten, and a check revealed a platoon or two of absentees from each company.

"Cawpril Badger is missing again. He got off at Paris."

"Fair enough," the Loot commented when

the Top brought in his report. "I expected it would be a lot worse. Who's running the guard?"

"Lieutenant Gregg."

"He's a good head—blind as a bat when he has to be."

Until long after midnight a light burned in the Colonel's tent where, with his adjutant and a shorthand expert who yawned considerably over his notes, a three-page typewritten order was being assembled for the company commanders.

The results of the Colonel's labors showed the next morning at an hour when the regimental surgeon, inventing a superfluous inspection, collided head-on with the Colonel's project whereby, on parade, each company of the Regiment would have an opportunity of listening to a long essay on a visionary dream called the Entente Cordiale.

French at a Glance showed that this pair of words was not a fancy drink, but long before the cross pull had destroyed the company commanders, both the Colonel and the regimental surgeon had surrendered their personal ambitions in favor of a brass-bound French officer whose life had been consecrated to the project of procuring a million dollars' worth of free pick and shovel work from the brave friends of war-torn France.

"The sewer, the latrine, the system of water and the road for wagons—she must be done all of a velocity," the Frenchman explained. "First, the farewell physical of the troop—then the inspection of his health—after that can come the words of friendship. That is the best—is it not so?"

It was not so, but nevertheless the Frenchman had his way.

"Assemble the companies and let the company commanders arrange the work details," the Colonel conceded. "My order relative to the necessity for establishing and maintaining the Entente with the French can be read at Retreat to-night. These first impressions are strongest, and the French are a sensitive people."

When the companies were lined up sometime after the news of the impending call for volunteers in the pick and shovel campaign had spread, it developed that nearly all of the men in the construction regiment were at that moment first-class clerks and stenographers. "There don't seem to be any roughnecks left in the outfit, Loot," Spike Randall reported.

"Forty ways. That simplifies everything. Every one of those shorthand experts gets himself a pick and a Number 2 muck-stick."

"What about the Gang? They didn't try to dodge anything."

"Hold 'em in camp for whatever soft jobs may come up. Maybe next time after the rest of the outfit get through manicuring that sewer job down at the Chinese camp by the river they won't try to duck the rough stuff."

At this moment an orderly from regimental headquarters appeared with a sheaf of orders and his little book. "Sign for 'em here, Lieutenant."

The Loot signed his name. Then, turning again to Spike, "I'll go down the hill with you and see what the job is as soon as you get the outfit equipped with its weapons. Hit the ball. Whatever the job is, let's get at it."

The first order on the stack was a summons

to all of the officers of the Regiment to report immediately at regimental headquarters. Here, when they were assembled, the Colonel addressed them briefly.

"Gentlemen," he said, "the officers of the Regiment have been honored by an invitation to dine to-night with the Mayor of Genimont-Lowzac, Monsieur Aubre Tiffonet. Ladies will be present. General Goizet-Diderot, the French commander of this region, will be the guest of honor. The General will be accompanied by his staff—perhaps ten or fifteen officers. We will assemble here to-night at eight o'clock. The quartermaster will provide transportation."

The Colonel, after a brief contemplative pause, launched forth into a résumé of the theme of the long order which he had composed during the previous night.

"Gentlemen, a house divided against itself must fall. This will be your first social contact with officers of the French army. Much depends upon these first impressions. I need not direct your attention to the fact that harmony of effort and coöperation are the fundamentals without which the union of the French and American forces must mean no added striking power against our common enemy. Friction and internal strife between the French and ourselves cannot fail to nullify much of the sacrifice which our country is making. You will conduct yourselves accordingly, and I trust that the event will strengthen the unity, will increase the bonds of friendship, existing between the United States and France."

The bonds of friendship, had the Colonel but known it, were receiving considerable attention from the newcomers even as he spoke. Patsy and Red Walker, seeking recreation in the midst of idleness, led half a dozen members of the Gang on a scouting expedition around the camp which resulted in an affiliation with a roving group of the local French population that had turned out to satisfy their curiosity concerning the Americans.

The Gang's vocabulary increased at the rate of a word a minute, and within an hour a good time was being had by all. "Listen, Cheery," Red Walker informed a comely girl, "you make a bokoo hit with me. Voo-lay-voo promenade pour vang rooge with me?"

Yes, of a certainty, if such were the wishes of the brave soldier.

"Listen, Sister, cut out that lookin' sideways at that bird. He ain't no B Company man. He don't belong—savvy?"

"Oui, M'sieur." It was remarkable how readily they understood English.

"Voo ist married, Cheery?" The questioner, playing safe, looked over the trail ahead before he ventured to march upon it.

"Non, M'sieur,"—that is to say, the fair one was as good as single, her husband being somewhere in the front-line trenches at the moment.

"Bong. Venay together avec me and j'ai will buy you une tray cher present . . . Leggo a her! What the hell! Me and her been walkin' for half an hour together. N'est-ce paw, Cheery?"

Yes to everything. Liberté, Egalité, Fraternité thrived mightily.

While the Gang enjoyed the companionship of congenial residents of the locality, the pseudo-stenographers who made up the work crew, having marched three or four miles down the hill from Genimont, came finally to the scene of their labors. Behind high walls stood forty acres of ammunition factories. Outside of these walls, strung along the bank of the Garonne, were long rows of huts wherein the French had housed three or four thousand Annamites who had been imported from the French colony.

These little brown men, many of them turned a bright yellow now, from the fumes of the acids which rose about them in the powder plant, were utterly indifferent to sanitary affairs.

Dogs and garbage littered the streets fronting the huts of the camp while, on the river bank behind the huts, festering filth invited dormant epidemics of disease.

Here, clearing away the accumulated filth, opening clogged sewers and repairing broken drains, labored the best construction talent imported from the United States.

Due to a slip in the program, only a third

of the work crew was equipped with tools.

The rest, standing by for a while, commented bitterly upon the nature of this first outlet for their patriotic energies; and then, having nothing better to do, the idlers were presently engaged in a verbal warfare with some of the little yellow Annamites who, encouraged by their droves of barking yellow dogs, screamed their resentment at the invasion of their premises.

One of them, gnashing a set of teeth blackened by betel-nut juice, was foolish enough to augment his tirade with a display of cutlery. It left him swimming in the turgid Garonne along with fifty of his fellows almost before his gleaming knife had hit the ground.

In more than one sense that section of the camp was cleaned out, and then, seeking further pleasurable relief from their distasteful labors, the work crew moved on downstream to another section of the camp where new adventures, along with new work, might be found.

In the meantime, on the hill around the Regiment's camp at Genimont, prowling in ever widening circles, Patsy and Fat, Jugger and Isadog, Tex, Rex and Mex, along with the rest of the students of romance, drifted finally out upon the broad highway which led down the hill to the pleasant river town of Lowzac where, as some bearer of glad tidings reported, "Bokoo beer can be had—and they got real ice."

In the Café de Poisson in Lowzac, helping papa behind the bar, labored the lovely Fifi. Sighting Fifi, "Stick here a moment, mon cheery," a member of the gang said to the girl who accompanied him, "I got to parley avec a man . . ."

But presently the deserter, discovering ice under Fifi's external warmth, sought his abandoned companion.

"Bokoo beer!"

Then, into the group, accompanied by an American girl, came the Uplifter. "Any time you boys get down to Bordeaux there are writing paper and cigarettes at our place. Come in whenever you're lonely and we'll try to cheer you up. When did you men get to France?"

"We just got in this week. Do you give them cigarettes away down at your place?"

The Uplifter smiled, but before he could speak the American girl answered. "We charge merely enough to make the place self-supporting," she said.

A frown settled on the male Uplifter's face. As a matter of fact, the uplift business was all new stuff to him. A man of wealth, a good American, volunteering for army service the first day after the United States sat into the Big Game, this Joe Miller had been turned down by the army surgeons on account of his age and his weight and his heart and his eyes and five or six other things.

"That's my name—honest," he explained to a member of the gang who, looking sideways at the American girl, was suddenly strong on introductions. "Joe Miller—but I didn't write the joke book. This is Miss Gay Winning—she can play the piano something fit to make your feet migrate! You retreat into the billiard room over there, Miss Winning, and tear into that piano I see against the wall. Maybe we have song birds with us."

Followed by a covey of music cravers, Miss Winning, the lady Uplifter, began her exit toward the piano in the billiard room of the Café de Poisson.

When she had left the group, Joe Miller heaved an honest sigh of relief, and then, "What'll you boys have?" he asked. To Fifi back of the bar, "Encore the beer if you please, Mademoiselle. Let these soldats Américains have anything they want and all of it they crave. Give me the check."

The Gang decided that here was a man who was white folks. Bitter experiences yet to come with other Uplifters were to stand black against the bright background of the party launched that afternoon by Joe Miller.

"Encore la beer, Fifi—bokoo beer!"

"Vang rooge!"

"Coonyak!"

The party began to become a real ruckus within the hour. Amateurs seeking to steady a local world which had suddenly begun to skid sideways every so often, fell back on footwork. Some of the health seekers, starting along the highway which led down the river bank toward the ammunition factories at Bassens, established contact with the outposts of the work crew.

In a flash the news spread down the line. "There's a grand celebration down at Lowzac. Free beer! Rich bird down there buyin' all the beer in the world for us soldiers."

Hearing this, lacking orders, fearing two or three vigilant officers, a bright sergeant destined for higher things formed the outfit and marched them in a column of squads to the scene of revelry.

Overflowing presently, the Café de Poisson spilled some of its customers into the open square of Lowzac around which five or six other cafés lived and had their being.

A complaint reached Joe Miller's sympathetic ears. "Joe, that bird over across the way there won't sell us anything."

"Hell, kid, show him to me. I'll bet a steel mill to a centime he'll sell us something. If he doesn't we'll buy his place and have him wrap it up. Come along and show him to me."

When six cafés around the public square

of Lowzac were flowing freely as all good cafés should, Joe Miller, millionaire patriot, stood alone for a moment and observed his handiwork.

"Goin' pretty good," he commented. "If I could only side-step Miss Vinegar-Face Gay Winning the rest of the afternoon I might put on a real show for the boys."

Late in the afternoon, when news of the celebration had spread throughout the district and when practically all of the Regiment had joined forces with the local French population in celebrating the cause of Liberté, Egalité, Fraternité, Joe Miller again sized up his handiwork and found it not so bad. "They didn't let me into their private and exclusive army, but the army seems to like me just the same," he protested to three or four sympathetic members of the Gang.

"You're damn right, Joe!"

"Show me the fella that wouldn't let you into the army and I'll break his damn neck."

"Joe, what's that uniform you got on—what's that three-cornered thing there on your arm?"

"That stands for Liberty, Equality, Fraternity. Whichever way you look at it you can see the point. Come on with me while we open up another keg."

While the next keg and yet other kegs were being opened by nearly all of the enlisted personnel of the Regiment, up the hill, after their Mess in a camp which seemed to be strangely deserted, the officers of the Regiment began their preparation for the dinner party to which they had been invited by the Mayor of Genimont.

The Loot devoted himself to a twenty-minute review of the French language, adding perhaps a dozen words to the meager vocabulary which remained as a residue of an abandoned ambition of his school days. "I can say yes and no, and that's about all," he confessed to the Captain of the Gang's company.

"That's twice as much as you'll need—say yes to everything," the Captain advised, "and when yes won't work, fall back on gestures. Personally, kid, I aim to lean heavy on a little sign language I learned down on the Arizona desert."

"That ought to get you by, Cap, with a casual wink thrown in at the right moment," some one called through a mask of lather. "Holy buzz saw, these razor blades got rusty!"

A cry for help from an adjoining section of the long building wherein the officers were quartered: "How in hell do you say the female word for beautiful—that is, how do you say, 'You are beautiful'?"

"You are cuckoo. You don't have to say it; just look it or hand her a bouquet of garlic."

"Think beautiful thoughts and the girls'll get you safe enough," another comforter assured the inquirer.

"To hell with all that sweet-scented jabber about love's young dream—what I want to know is when do we eat and how?"

"You'll eat plenty. The banquet will be a mile long and six feet deep in the finest line of drinks you ever tasted."

"Lead me to it! Where's all that transportation the feeble quartermaster was to have rounded up?"

"Here it comes. Never mind the guard. All out, you birds, and don't drink out of the finger bowls."

At nightfall the great and beautiful château which was the residence of Aubre Tiffonet became the setting for a brilliant scene. Beautiful women and brave men of France, arriving late, greeted the American officers who had come early to avoid the rush around the flowing bowl.

Equipped with an average of three French phrases apiece, and forbearing to parade them more than once or twice for the edification of their fair companions, the younger officers of the Regiment milled rapidly among the ladies, seeking to favor each one with a full list of compliments.

"I gaze upon you charming to-night."

"I am very fortunate for you to make my acquaintance."

"May you wish have me with a cocktail."

Twenty-four ladies meant a perfect score of twenty-four appetizing drinks, and to the credit of the Regiment it is recorded that some of the gentlemen made perfect scores.

On the crest of the seventh wave an owl-eyed major came stiffly to attention before the Loot, who was at the moment conversing fluently in some unknown language with the lovely niece of Aubre Tiffonet.

"Lieutenant," the major inquired, "when do we eat? . . . Bong nude, Señorita."

"How droll, is it not?"

"Ah oui, mon cheery," the Loot began, but his finer phrases were smothered by a sudden silence which spread through the brilliant throng.

"The General!"

Announced with due formality by a cheer leader in livery, M. le Général Goizet-Diderot rendered a graceful salute to the company from where he stood immediately behind his stomach in the arched doorway of the great room. At the rotund General's side, completing the picture of a side view of an old-fashioned bicycle with the little wheel and the big wheel, stood Miss Gay Winning. Miss Gay had side-stepped the Lowzac ruckus in favor of the bigger and better things of life. "Hello, people!" Miss Gay called to the company, and then to the General, who was her escort, "Oh, Guzzy, isn't this just the damn *love*liest party!"

Forthwith, after five, ten or fifteen drinks had splashed into the ponderous Commander of the Region, dinner was announced. After a momentary period of confusion during which the younger officers of the Regiment sought to side-step a sudden epidemic of elderly ladies and dignified aunties who had unexpectedly appeared on the scene, the company paraded into a dazzling crystal cave and sat down to dinner.

The Loot closed one eye and read an engraved wine list which lay on the table before him. "A threat or a promise," he thought, "but either way I'm sure programmed for a flood of likker."

From across the table his Captain, reading a duplicate of the wine list, spoke quickly to the Loot. "Never mind the cockeyed guard! Boy, this looks like the best war we ever fought. . . . Here's luck!"

At the Café Poisson in Lowzac, Tex, Rex

and Mex batted the music for Miss Gay Winning after her departure, putting on an impromptu entertainment which presently subsided into a riotous dance.

Here was jazz! Heavy hands banged the keyboard of the swaying piano, and then outside the Café a skidding automobile delivered a cargo of band instruments. The music changed from bad to worse and from worse to a wild blaring rhythm that galvanized the oldest native inhabitant who heard it.

Hilaire, Plutarque, Ovide, Corneille, rheumatic and ancient veterans of the Lowzac Fire Department, reacted in spite of rheumatism and were dancing presently with French flappers of seventy and less.

A yowling blast from a locomotive whistle punctuated the blaring music and under the booming of the big bass drum came the rumble of a northbound train.

Along one side of the open square of Lowzac, bounded by the elevated structure of the railway above, and by a row of round tables fronting the Café Chemin de Fer, the dancers looked upward at the incoming train, noting that it was crowded with French soldiers. Then, amid a frantic exchange of greetings between the traveling troops and the dancers in the open space below them, the revel was resumed.

Contributing his bit to the gayety, an envious French soldier leaned far out of the doorway of his car. After taking careful aim he dropped an empty wine bottle fair upon the cluttered top of a table below him.

He scored a five; and in addition, without knowing it, he had fired the first gun in a new war.

Around the table when the bottle crashed in its center sat half a dozen of the Gang. "What the hell!"

Plans for retaliation and revenge bloomed on the instant, but, save for a harmless return volley of beer bottles, revenge at the moment was not enjoyed because the train was under way and the originator of the quaint jest could not be located among the derisive Frenchmen who grinned and grimaced from each passing car.

Except for the members of the Gang

around the bombarded table the encounter passed almost unnoticed, save that the station master, telephoning from his elevated perch above the square of Lowzac, relayed distorted news of the affair to his fellows in Bordeaux. "Upon the railway carriages the soldiers of America have, with empty bottles and other missiles, committed an assault."

Enough. The second section of the troop train, leaving Bordeaux twenty minutes later, carried four hundred men, most of whom were resolved to avenge the insult offered to their comrades during the brief moment while the train halted above the throng at Lowzac. "The egg, the vegetable, regardless of expense, the discarded sock—these will serve for the barrage! How admirable!"

While the attacking forces were accumulating ammunition and while their intended victims were making up for lost time in the square at Lowzac, Aubre Tiffonet, addressing the dinner party assembled in his château, launched forth on a speech calculated to cement a little more firmly the ties which bound America to France.

The Mayor, accomplished in languages, spoke in what he thought was English. He reviewed the plight of France, he echoed the call which had gone forth for help, he dwelt at length upon the demonstrated ability, the unquestioned courage of America. . . .

M. le Général Goizet-Diderot, sitting in the place of honor, held his bulging stomach in his lap and struggled to stay awake.

"For Gawd sake when is he coming to the toast?" An agitated brother officer whispered the hoarse question to the Loot.

"Before this insane ambition for the career political claimed him, dear Uncle Tiffonet was never like this," the charming niece of the Mayor confided to her dinner companion, who nodded his head to indicate a complete understanding of her words.

"Ah oui, Sister, oui, oui, mon cheery."

Winding up for his supreme effort, the Mayor indulged in a preliminary gesture which knocked over two long-necked bottles of wine at his right, and then: "I get the honor of to propose the health in that distinguished what you have said in bon mot the

Roughneck Rider, and of himself a true friend to France, none the less Woodrow Roosevelt, President of the United States———"

"Psss-s-s-t—Wilson! Wilson!"

"—who preceded that thrice amiable M'sieur Wilson, the present holder of that high office!"

The amendment carried, and the Americans present drank two drinks apiece. In some confusion, justly doubting the adroitness with which he had masked his ignorance of American politics, the Mayor sat down.

There followed a pause during which the younger American officers snaked another two or three drinks apiece; and then, with a smile in his kindly eyes, the Colonel of the Engineer Regiment nodded to one of his officers, a major who possessed no small talent for Bourbon and its contingent oratory.

The major got to his feet with the assistance of a tactful servant. For a little while the major stood gazing, owl-like, as if hypnotized, straight before him into the round red face of General Goizet-Diderot.

The face of the General appeared to be an obstacle to the major's oratory.

Then suddenly, while the company waited for the flood of eloquence, the major hiccuped slightly and pointed his finger at the red face of the ponderous General Goizet-Diderot. In good voice the major began his speech: "Look at that fat bird—he's sound asleep! . . . I thank you!"

The major sat down.

"How droll these Americans, is it not?"

Taking up the speech where the disabled major had left off, the Colonel did the best he could, while, from the far end of the banquet hall a troup of six lieutenants, suddenly realizing that they were trained bears, slid to the floor and began an exit on hands and knees toward the drawing-room adjoining. Presently the Colonel's speech was accompanied by strains of music, while a singing voice which was suddenly choked to silence announced that there would be a hot time in the old town that night.

Surrendering to his personal desires, to the dictates of common sense and to overwhelming odds, the Colonel picked up his oration and carried it boldly to the place where the President of France waited eagerly for his bit of tommy rot.

"Here's luck!" a junior officer volunteered while the toast was being drunk. "Hooray for us and France!"

The music from the drawing-room swelled to a louder strain. The dancing consisted of a high-pressure course of instruction wherein a score of the loveliest ladies in France learned a lot less than they craved to know about the style of dancing just then in vogue in the United States.

By bending his beribboned chest over and above his stomach, General Goizet-Diderot was enabled to get near enough to the hypnotizing little Miss Gay Winning to accompany her through the contortions of a daily dozen. "Come home or writhe! Hoop-la!"

Faintly echoing the dizzy General's exclamation of delight, far away at Lowzac the locomotive of the second section of the French troop train whistled for that station.

"Let your aim be made with a deliberation,

my braves," a platoon commander advised his comrades on the train, and then, firing at will after the first volley, the vegetable barrage of revenge was hurled by eager patriots toward the Americans in the open square below.

After the first flight of missiles had been launched, quickly realizing the nature of the attack, the Engineers came back with an impetuous enthusiasm that evened the score with the second volley.

Beer bottles, hurtling upward, moaned plaintive notes from their open necks and showered broken glass upon the occupants of the train.

With the honors even after the first minute, seeking to quell the riot, here and there in the open square peace-loving Frenchmen laid hands upon aroused Americans and then, as the troop train pulled out to the tune of the station master's penny whistle, the second phase of the Battle of Lowzac had begun.

Observing this, "Mon Dieu!" the spying station master exclaimed. "The combat internationale!" He leaped to his telephone. "Allo! Allo!" he began, and, following a

Entente Cordiale 99

vituperative torrent poured into the ears of the exchange operators, he was connected presently with police headquarters in Bordeaux. "Reserves to Lowzac! Rioting has begun which is three times terrible. Make haste!"

This accomplished, the Chef de Gare sought the aid of more appropriate authority over the copper circuit which led to the château of M. Aubre Tiffonet.

To that personage, "A deplorable affair is approaching its crisis in this place of your jurisdiction!" Explaining the nature of the affair, "The citizens of Lowzac are engaged in combat with the troops American," the station master announced. "It is three times plus terrible! Summon the commanding colonel of the Americans before his men are overwhelmed——"

In a bright circle of light cast by a street lamp the Chef de Gare saw one of the threatened Americans plow his way through a group of his French opponents, leaving behind him half a dozen prostrate forms. . . .

"Ah,—the boxing! The Americans make

to kill with the fist, Monsieur Tiffonet! Summon their commanding officer, I implore you, before his men are destroyed!"

In some haste and suffering from no little apprehension, Monsieur le Maire sought the Colonel of the Regiment. "We will go at once to Lowzac if you please, mon Colonel," the Mayor said with some formality.

The Colonel considered taking an escort with him and then, thinking better of it, he bowed to the Mayor of Genimont-Lowzac. "At your pleasure, sir," the Colonel agreed, and a moment later, in the low, rakish limousine enjoyed by the Mayor at the expense of the munition works, the two gentlemen began their dash to the scene of conflict.

For a while along the level river bank the automobile ran smoothly. Then, failing to function, the car sneezed harshly. Deep within its hot mechanism a fife-and-drum corps began to sound, and the car stopped.

The Mayor's chauffeur, cheerful and optimistic, judged that one little minute would be sufficient time in which to repair his gargling pet. The little minute lengthened into five, into ten, into twenty, while with increased formality marking his silence the Mayor sat in one corner of the car and devoted himself to turning purple in the darkness, laboring with superhuman effort to control an exploding vocabulary of naughty, naughty cuss words.

Near him, braced comfortable into the other corner of the limousine the Colonel drew evenly upon a long and comforting cigar, the while reviewing the phrases of the three-page order which he had composed in an effort toward strengthening the justly celebrated Entente Cordiale.

Some minutes later, when the Colonel's cigar was half consumed and while the fuming chauffeur had begun to blame a long line of paternal ancestors for accomplishing the sorry event of his birth, the Bordeaux police reserves arrived upon the battlefield in the square at Lowzac.

It appeared that some imagination had been injected into the station master's description of the riot. About the square, French girls were dancing gayly with the American soldiers while in the brightly lighted cafés which edged the open space enthusiastic groups of Frenchmen drank to the health of the Americans amid cheers and loud song and broken phrases of two garbled languages.

From the Café Poisson, blaring into the night out of the brass throats of a dozen band instruments came music and discord which thrilled the calloused hearts of the amiable Bordeaux police reserves,—and they fell.

In the billiard room adjoining the bar of the Café Poisson, on an impromptu throne which had been erected upon a billiard table, sat Joe Miller. The Uplifter's perspiring brow upheld a silken crown while draped about him clustered a concentrated group of feminine youth and beauty.

"I'm old man Bacchus!" the Uplifter announced catching sight of some of the police reserves who had entered the café. "Give these noble hen-darmeys a drink. Open some more champagne,—hooray for France!"

When the echoes of the cheering were drowned in gurgles, the ancient Plutarque, enjoying the moral support of Hilaire, Victoire, Ovide, Corneille, Bartolemy, veterans of the Lowzac Fire Department, raised another cheer for the land of the strangers. "Huzzash pour l'Amérique!" piped old Plutarque, holding his gnashing false teeth in place by means of an extended thumb. "Hooroosh pour lesh Américains!"

Then, while a gratifying response answered him, the old man removed his false teeth and applied himself diligently to the task of emptying a bottle of champagne without the aid of any intermediate glassware.

In upon this scene, some time after the Bordeaux police reserves had enjoyed their seventh round of drinks, marched the Mayor of Genimont-Lowzac, M. Aubre Tiffonet, together with the Colonel commanding the Regiment of Engineers.

For a fleeting moment the pair gazed upon the scene before them, and then, in a smiling response to a bellowed invitation from old Joe Bacchus Miller, the Mayor and the Colonel pledged each other's health with a bottle of champagne and, bowing to the company, withdrew to where the limousine awaited them. The fog of formality dissolved into the airs of the riotous night.

"Return to my residence," the Mayor directed. Then, countermanding his order, he got out of the car and hurried back to the Café Poisson. He returned a moment later carrying two open and foaming bottles of champagne, one of which he presented to the Colonel.

"Permit me, my Colonel, to have the goddam honor of drink to your health . . . Whuf! . . . It is, as you say in your most admirable language, always making weather when goddam good boys get altogether." To the chauffeur, "Hasten, my child—return to my residence where as host I have been so neglectful."

Before he entered into the scene of revelry at his château, M. Aubre Tiffonet whispered some hurried directions concerning a reserve store of champagne which he had laid down twelve years before. "Not one case, fool!" he replied to his servant's question, "—a dozen cases—six dozen cases—all of it,—as long as these brave gentlemen take pleasure in its bouquet." Then, arm in arm with the Colonel, the Mayor returned to the company in his drawing-room.

The two gentlemen halted for a moment in the doorway of the main salon.

Before them, perspiring freely and dying a martyr's death, the red-faced, ponderous General Goizet-Diderot, electrified by some momentary and miraculous vigor, whirled through the violent termination of an Apache dance with the sprightly Miss Gay Winning, who, in complete abandon, had discarded most of her early training and part of her costume under the spell of the wild music of the dance.

At the conclusion of the exhibition General Goizet-Diderot sat down with his stomach in his lap, giving place to an enthusiastic company commander who, light on his feet, slapped the floor with a preliminary patter of soft-shoe dancing which spread spontaneously until it reached the Colonel of the Regiment.

"Boys will be boys," the Colonel reflected. Then, gracefully removing his spurs and regretting the slight impediment to perfection imposed by his polished boots, he took up the pattering footwork which had developed in his old Kentucky homeland. Forthwith he afforded his delighted audience a whirlwind exhibition of what a young man of sixty could do when he spread himself.

"Hot dam! Look at the Colonel go! Boy, he's buildin' a fire with each foot."

The Loot, forgetting his French, poured his admiring criticism of the Colonel's performance into the little pink ears of the niece of Aubre Tiffonet. "Lord, Lord, lady—was fancy hoofing a dewdrop, our Colonel is the Mississip'. Sand the rail—I'm slipping. C'mon, baby, let's go!"

The Mayor's niece felt a strong arm about her waist, and a moment later she was deep in the mazes of the dizzy jazz whose fury, inspired by the Colonel's example, had claimed every member of the applauding company.

In the cold gray dawn, riding up the hill to Genimont in the limousine placed at his service by his admiring host, the Colonel spoke briefly to his adjutant who sat beside him.

"The order which you suggested relative to the necessity for promoting the Entente Cordiale—if you have sent it to the company commanders, cancel it! If it hasn't gone out, tear it up! Forget it! And in the future, Captain, avoid all such superfluous details."

Chapter 4

First to Fight—for Cupid

IN the winter rains of sunny France the Regiment dissolved, and the several companies found themselves facing professional problems not unworthy of their abilities. Docks, railway yards and a great storage depot designed to hold canned salmon and other military delicacies for an army of a million stomachs claimed the attention of the Engineers.

Before the first shipments of dead goldfish had begun to bulge their tin caskets, the Gang selected a lucky number and won a storage depot which spread across the blueprints a mile wide and long enough to reach well into the next war.

Executive talent, superintendents and foremen, drawn from the Gang's personnel, formed the nucleus of an organization which obtained its labor from every available source. Pioneers and old-timers on the job, the Gang were presently surrounded by a camp which sheltered some thousands of construction men—negro stevedore troops, German prisoners of war, civilian forces from Spain and an ever-changing contingent of various transient boarders of the A. E. F.

First discovering what work was to be done, the Gang began to do it. Then when their great engine of industry worked a little more smoothly after the acute shortage of labor and material had been overcome, one by one the old-timers, roving on their infrequent holidays between Bordeaux and Libourne, did their best to establish, mid pleasures and palaces, some of the comforts of home, sweet home.

True enough, where the male population of the land about them did their bit now and then to stress the ties of the Entente in mercenary matters, but without malice aforethought—blowing up occasional fixed prices right in the purchaser's face—the Gang's romantic relationship with the feminine youth and beauty of their environment left nothing much to be desired. For a while they enjoyed a monopoly in their field, but with the delayed arrival of later waves of the million men in O. D. who had sprung to arms overnight, the competition became keener and it became necessary to employ something more tangible than fermented phrases of affection to maintain the ground gained in the garden of romance.

"Aw, listen, mon cheery, vous do not need no new chapeau. Tray jolie maint'nong. And listen, cheery—them artillery hommes est par bong. Vous git me, Sister?"

The maintenance item became a crucial problem. Compared to the upkeep, the first cost of true and lasting friendships was negligible. In vain did the Gang concentrate on translating the higher flights of impassioned oratory. Words were met with sad sweet smiles.

"Listen, cheery, you look bokoo more jolie not avec jewelry. Venay away from that window—vous par need that wrist watch."

At a dark hour when a regiment of infantry

equipped with three months' back pay invaded the harem and threatened to overthrow a hundred established institutions which had thrived up to that moment on nothing more substantial than love's old sweet song and other verbal considerations, wagoner Tex Miller, working overtime at a lathe in the repair shop, hit upon an expedient which did much to strengthen the weakened ties which bound the lady friends of the Gang to their true but blue soldats.

After a highly unsatisfactory evening with Mademoiselle Julie Renan, her widowed mother, three elderly aunts and an assortment of grandparents, "Tray bong, cheery," Tex had conceded. "J'ai will bring you une jolie ring pour la finger to-morrow night. Comprenday?"

Returning to the repair shop, somewhat fed up on finicky femmes, Tex sawed off a short section of a round brass rod an inch in diameter and clamped it in the chuck of a lathe which formed part of the shop's equipment. He started the lathe and within ten minutes the spirals of gleaming metal curling from the cutting tool had laid bare a bright yellow band which Tex bored to fit the third finger of the charming Julie's hand. "Get me a piece of that emery cloth," Tex directed one of the bystanders, "an old piece that's smooth."

"What you makin'?"

"I'm riggin' up a roller bearin' for a high roller," Tex stated, and then, withholding nothing: "If you got to know, it's a ring for a girl. I aim to ring a belle before all this infantry gang that got in last week busts up an old friendship."

"Make me one, will you, Tex? Fifi like to clawed my arm off yesterday in front of a jewelry store, beggin' me to get her one."

"Tex, as long as you got that long bar of brass in that lathe, go ahead and cut off a few more of them rings." Another bystander of the night shift seemed to realize that opportunity was knocking at his door.

Within the next two days each member of the Gang had equipped himself with a collection of rings in assorted sizes which needed only a few swipes on the rough sleeve of an

O. D. blouse to make them gleam as brightly as fine gold. "Raus mitt those infantry guys—mighty funny how all the femmes around here seem to prefer us Engineers to everybody, even if those other birds have got bokoo francs."

From this traffic in munitions of romance, after the experiment had demonstrated its success and had become a settled industry, Tex profited financially to the extent of one franc per ring.

"Nix on that pay-day stuff!" he remonstrated when a ring-craver sought credit. "Either you come across a franc a throw or else you can rustle your jewelry from some place else. If you haven't got the jack why don't you go borrow it some place? Get some from the Loot or hit Nick the Greek for it. He dealt himself rich last night in the black-jack game."

"I owe the Loot thirty francs now, Tex, and that louse of a Nick ain't lending his losers nothing. I got cleaned for eight francs in that game myself last night."

"On your way, boy—I don't want to get

hard or nothing, but cash is my motto. You birds on the free list used up an eight-foot bar of that brass without nothin' coming my way, and from now on this business is C. O. D. cash!"

Something had changed in Tex Miller's make-up. "What the hell d'ya suppose can be eatin' that bird, gittin' hard like a M. P.—how does he git that way?"

As a matter of fact, enjoying the social advantages derived from a heavy purse, Tex had got that way from the effects of recurrent fits of gazing into the immediate future while suffering from incidental delusions of grandeur. "Combien francs can deux people such as une homme and une femme live on around here, keeping a maisong?" he asked the vivacious Julie, indulging in a daydream wherein prattling children played around the little cabin door.

Tex's French in this instance was too deep for his companion. She changed the subject to a string of compliments concerning Nick the Greek. "The sergeant Nick, how gallant and how successful! Within a few days he tells me he is to be promoted to become an officer. Already he has the leggings of leather."

"Listen, Julie, vous lay off that snake. In the first place he's a buck private and in the second place he's got no more chance of being an officer than our mascot goat!"

Nevertheless, with a sudden and suspicious proficiency in English, Julie maintained that among other admirable qualities Nick the Greek was a gallant and entertaining dinner companion. "To-night he make me the dinner in the grand ville of Bordeaux with the biftek, with the plenty sugar in the pocket, with the champagne to drink it. Voilà, M'sieur Tex—let us speak no more words of Meestaire Nick."

Tex spoke no more words of Nick Pappas, the snakelike Greek who went about deceiving young girls as to his military status, but to himself he marshaled a list of phrases couched in a heartfelt burst of profanity which required almost superhuman effort to withhold.

Tex and Julie had been enjoying a promenade, a march of freedom away from relatives and other pests, but now abruptly Julie's escort did an about-face and started for her residence.

"Listen, cheery, j'ai take you to your maisong, and then—bong nuit! Vous can ramble avec that Nick diable, s'il vous plaît, but I et vous parti toot sweet."

At the entrance to Mademoiselle Julie's house, after a silence which had lasted for the last hundred yards of the return journey, "Au revoir forever, cheery," and then, confining himself to honest English, the while maintaining on his face a bitter smile, "Throw that ring I give you in the ash can for all I give a damn. Good night!"

At the moment when Tex suffered most acutely from the pangs of despised love, Alexander Nikolaus Pappaloupolous, or more briefly Nick Pappas as indicated on his service record, or "Nick the Greek" as the Gang knew him, was gloating at a bit of information relayed to him by the Loot, for whom he worked as dog-robber whenever his blackjack game and his "barber shop" could spare him.

Undoubtedly Nick the Greek had a way with women. This the Gang conceded. In addition, Nick was a fair barber and as such he was entitled to his rations, according to the older members of the Gang to whom three shaves a week were essential to comfort.

After a discouraging series of experiments calculated to land the ever-apologetic Nick in the right job, "I'll take him for my striker," the Loot decided. "He isn't worth a damn anywhere else, so he can keep things rigged up for me." The Loot was just then averaging sixteen hours of labor per day, and here and there Nick the Greek was able to do his bit for the big construction job by doing his bit for the Loot.

The Gang conceded that in little things Nick the Greek watched the game and was thoughtful and observing. "Johnny-at-the-rat-hole with hot coffee for the Loot when he comes in wore out at midnight."

"He's a good enough dog-robber, all right, but you can't make me believe anybody can beat payin' nineteen every doggone time in a blackjack game without readin' the backs of them cards."

"Another thing—he's gettin' too damn pertickler about will he shave us boys or not since the Loot made him dog-robber. Try to get a shave off him and he's just then got to do this or that or somethin' else for the Lieutenant."

"I seen him in Bordeaux the other day all shined up, wearin' the Loot's old leggin's—I had a good mind to sic a M. P. on him, struttin' around like a jigadier brindle tellin' all them dames he was a ossifer."

"Well, you got to hand it to him fer one thing," a fourth observer conceded. "Except fer Corporal Badger that's been A. W. O. L. every time we had any hard work ever since we left New York, that bird is fightin' a mighty soft war. Bokoo femmes, bokoo francs, bokoo passes—he's got it on us forty ways. You got to hand it to him, I tell you. That snake lit soft."

While the jury was out, Nick the Greek, seeking a pass to Bordeaux for the following night, fell back on the never-failing condiment trick which was practiced so extensively in the A. E. F. by the dog-robbing tribe. "The cook he needs some mushroom sauce and some other things for to make your rations taste better, Lieutenant," the snake announced. His voice seemed to be melancholy with sadness at the thought of his Lieutenant having to suffer for all the comforts of home merely because a war was raging. "If Lieutenant could give me the pass to Bordeaux to-morrow evening I would rush to Bordeaux and rush back with everything."

"All right." The Loot was thinking of sixteen hundred other matters, each one twice as important as a mingled cargo of condiments and dog-robbers combined. In spite of this, devoting another moment to Nick the Greek, "There's an order out making everybody cut his hair short," he announced. "Little over an inch in front, Nick. Remember it when you cut anybody's hair."

"Lieutenant, yes, sir." Forthwith, broadcasting the order after Retreat and embellishing it with specifications not in the original text: "Every man has to get his hair cut an inch and a quarter short. That is a new order from General Pershing that the Lieutenant just told me."

Seekers after truth, accosting the Lieutenant, verified the general burden of the dog-robber's announcement. "We got to get our hair cut short, Lieutenant?"

"I guess so. There's an order out about it somewhere."

Thereafter for three hours, functioning in his intermittent capacity as the Gang's barber, the snake Nick enjoyed a rush of trade that brought in a substantial addition to his blackjack profits.

"To-morrow night the little girl shall live on the fat of the land," he gloated, and, continuing to gloat, "Tell everybody General Pershing says come here and get his hair cut right away," he instructed each of his departing customers.

"To hell with that stuff."

Counteracting the burst of prosperity which threatened Nick the Greek, an ingenious member of the Gang spread an alarm wherein the horrors of barber's itch, sloughing away of the scalp, leprosy and general decomposition of the human body were set forth in the vivid language employed by advertising saviors of physical wrecks.

"Not me—I don't go near that Greek bird to get my hair cut. Come on down to Tex Miller's machine shop. He's got an electric horse's clippers in that wagoner's outfit of his and they cut your hair twice as fast anyhow. I don't take no chances getting barber's itch and everything off of those old combs Nick has."

In the tonsorial emporium of Nick Pappas the horn of plenty sounded one dying toot and was silent.

The silence was golden for Tex Miller, where, from the whirring blades of the horse clippers, hair cascaded from the heads of the Gang until, according to orders, it left them bald within an inch and a quarter of their skulls, with bare streaks here and there where the clippers had slipped.

The stampede ended with money enough in Tex Miller's possession to make him think seriously of abandoning the trade in brass rings in favor of his new vocation. If nothing else could be said for it, hair cutting was at least free from contingent tragedies involving fickle and faithless ladies who dined with snakes such as Nick Pappas.

A good man being hard to find and harder to hold in spite of America's contribution to the shortage, when Mme. Louise Renan became informed of her daughter's interest in Nick the Greek she lavished a wealth of sound advice, born of experience, upon the fickle Mlle. Julie.

"M'sieur Tex Miller, he is an honest man, and you are a little fool to desert him for this black-haired lackey to uncouth officers. Your father, alas, resembled Nick the Greek, and never for a moment could I trust him. True enough he was a man of substance, but only because of the wealth I brought him at the time of our marriage. Never could I be sure of one single thing about your papa—except that he was ardent in his love."

Rendering justice to her dear departed, Mme. Renan reserved to herself the bitter realization that her husband's ardor in affairs romantic had been disseminated over an area wide enough to deprive it of most of its impact wherever a single target of his affection had been concerned.

"M'sieur Tex, on the other hand, is blond and he is honest and of a stature how magnificent. With the fingers of one hand he could destroy a dozen sleek, pomaded barbers such as this Nick the Greek."

"True enough, my mamma," Mlle. Julie returned. "But what would you have me do —in my pride can I encourage a great blond bear who instructed me in English at the anguished moment of our parting to throw his pledge of love into the ash can?"

Seeking to end the ordeal, Mlle. Julie permitted herself to indulge in a tear of half-sincere regret. The older woman abandoned her lecture. "There, my angel," she comforted. "May the devil take all men! We have wealth enough to permit us to remain aloof from these heartbreaking savages. Dry your tears, my child, and smile. The end of love is the beginning of wisdom, and I tell

First to Fight—for Cupid 125

you that naught but distress lies beyond the doors of a man's heart."

Later in the day, realizing the quality of deceit contained in the last phrases of her advice to her daughter, Mme. Renan adopted a course dictated by common sense. She resolved to interview the blond and thrice-admirable Tex Miller in an effort to replace the leaden gray of love's young dream with a lighter tint which should presently match the petals of the rose.

"They's a dame out there lookin' fer you, Tex," a scout at the door of the repair shop informed the brass ring magnate early in the following afternoon.

"I'm off of dames f'r life,—to hell with 'em! Tell her I sent my laundry already, if that's what she's after."

"This ain't no washerwoman, big boy. She's a peach of a looker and she's ridin' in a pony cart. Maybe she wants to get her horse half-soled or something. Go on out and see her—there may be francs in it, and God knows I need 'em if you don't, since that snake of a Nick cleaned me at blackjack again. I'll half-sole her horse,—tell her,—for a franc a hoof."

"I'll look her over," Tex conceded. He turned his work at the lathe over to the franc-craver. "Take a finishin' cut of a sixty-fourth off of this pin after she runs out—and keep the soapy water runnin' on that tool. She's cuttin' hard."

Laboring under the stress imposed by an imaginary picture of the affairs incident to the champagne banquet at which the Greek snake had entertained the heartless Julie, toward all womankind at that moment Tex Miller's heart presented an armored surface as hard as steel. He made his exit from the repair shop and confronted the peach of a looker who was seated in her pony cart.

"My goodness—why, bonjour, Madame Renan! Como tally vour health?"

The satisfactory state of Mme. Renan's health, it developed, was second only to her delight in seeing the brave Tex Miller after what had seemed an interminable period of three days since his last visit with Mlle. Julie.

First to Fight—for Cupid 127

"The affairs of war, they have engage you, is it not?"

"Ah, oui—bokoo work."

A passing frown darkened Tex Miller's countenance at Mme. Renan's preliminary exposition of the desolation which her daughter suffered by reason of the thrice-agreeable gentleman's prolonged absence from the Renan establishment.

How they missed his laughter and the advantages in the matter of accomplishing command of that most difficult language, Mme. Renan deplored,—the English as she was spoken; the terpsichorean delights purveyed by that how plaintive yet how sweet violin of the accomplished soldier.

Only that morning at the time of soup had it been necessary to comfort the distressed grandpère Renan, who longed for the soothing strains of the violin in the masterful hands of M'sieur Tex Miller—for the exhilarating melody of—what you call?—the "Turkey in the Straw," the inspiring M'sieur McGinty who went down to the bottom of the sea, and the "How Dry I Am" solo wherein "nobody geeve a good goddam."

Back in the repair shop Tex Miller's helper made the finishing cut on the crank pin in the lathe. He tried it with a micrometer gauge and set about giving the pin a polish which would leave it within a thousandth of an inch one way or the other of perfection.

During all of this the absent Tex, oblivious to the march of time, remained at Mme. Renan's side until a booming whistle midway of the warehouse project abruptly recalled the hypnotized one to the realities of life.

He bade the lady in the pony cart a lingering adieu in phrases which he realized were totally inadequate for the finer sentiments which language might convey. "J'ai suis tray regret for party avec vous maint'nong," he affirmed. And then, "Absolute-mong, Madame—j'ai veneer to your maisong après eaty petit supper ce soir . . . ah oui, j'ai portay mong violin. Absolute-mong. Au revoir, mon cheery Louise."

These last words softly, being as yet uncertain of his ground.

When Mme. Renan had left, returning to the repair shop where his helper had diverted the soapy water for the purposes of personal ablution, to himself, "Saa-y-y boy! . . . Holy suffering side-stepped grief—I been blind as a bat. She's got it on that finicky femme of a daughter forty ways from the jack."

"What's eatin' you—what you mumblin' about?" The helper, noting the wild light in Tex Miller's eyes, observing the wide gulf which suddenly yawned between Tex Miller's mind and the pleasing reality of the Mess Call which had blared, fired a question at his companion. "What's eatin' on you, big boy?"

"Nothin' eatin' on me," Tex returned, struggling back to normalcy. "Where's that resin you borrowed from the blacksmith? I got to get that fiddle bow of mine back into shape. This here damp air has like to spoiled it."

After supper, when the fiddle bow had been attended to, seeking a pass for the evening, Tex smiled a negative to several invitations to engage in local diversions of the moment and walked directly to company headquarters. In an unexpected encounter with the Lieutenant the pass-craver collided head on with one of those annoying changes of program which so often gummed up the private and personal schedules projected by victims of the S. O. S.

"Order came in from Base Headquarters in the evening mail that ropes you into a temporary life of ease," the Loot informed him. "Ever since you and Rex and Mex played at that 'Y' show the Uplifters have been on your trail. I busted their game a couple of times, but they've got all three of you birds rounded up this time and I guess there's no way of beating the deal. A little play won't hurt you any."

"What's the deal, Lieutenant?"

"The General seems to think that a tuneful trio that can dish out plenty of jazz will save bokoo life in the camps around the Base. There's three hundred thousand men in the Base and from the General's order it looks like half of 'em are pining away for the lack of a little vaudeville—anyhow, Tex, Rex and Mex, violin, banjo and saxophone experts, are scheduled for a triumphal tour. Transportation by the quartermaster and eat where you can find it."

"Lord, Lieutenant, that's a terrible mess for a man to get himself into." His projected theater of action, wherein the charming Mme. Louise Renan played her part opposite the hero, crashed suddenly to dust. "With all this new motive power comin' into the yard, I don't see how I can get away from the repair shop to go fiddlin' around with any uplift vaudeville outfit."

"Neither do I, Tex, but we're too close to the throne to duck the job. The General has remembered you three birds ever since the night you played at the 'Y.' He had me on the phone half an hour after the order got here and reinforced it with some language. The old boy is a shark on detail."

"I'll tell the cockeyed world he is—maybe he'd let me go if I'd sprain my arm or something."

"Forget it. If you three birds mean half as much to the outfits that'll hear you as you have to the Gang, the chances are they'll make you kings of France. Hop to it and come on home when the job is done. You ought to get back here in two or three weeks. Highball to-morrow morning, and if you get in a jam I'll be on this end of the wire."

"Fair enough, Lieutenant — I'll ride through with it, but get me back to the Gang as quick as you can."

Forthwith, disheartened at the temporary prospect of roving around apart from the Gang and from Mme. Renan, Tex sought that lady, bearing his violin in fulfillment of his promise of the afternoon.

His music that night, as much as his manner, conveyed some doleful portent which presently elicited from the observing Mme. Louise a question as to its cause. "Why is it, M'sieur Tex, that on this evening you play your music of such a sadness?"

Trying to tell it all, Tex delivered an explanation, and his manner conveyed far more to his sympathetic questioner than lay in his jumbled words. "J'ai necessaire parti avec vous pour tray weeks. J'ai and mon amis make music pour bokoo soldats—pour tout le monde of soldats around here."

Alas—but there would be glad returning, was it not?

To be sure there would be a returning. "J'ai retournay to vous toot sweet après finnay music."

Smiling faintly though clouds veiled his rising star of hope, Tex accepted from the fair hand of Madame Louise a crystal cup of rare liqueur.

"To your continued happiness, my brave M'sieur Tex, and to a safe returning. . . ."

"Ah oui, mon cheery—drink hearty," the doleful one replied, absorbing the stirrup cup with an appreciative cluck. Then the quick pain of parting. "Au revoir, mon dear cheery."

Hell! Why was the A. E. F. so lousy with regrettable farewells!

On the following morning, traveling to Bordeaux in an asthmatic motor, the trio entered upon a tour of entertainment which lasted a week over the schedule.

During all of this time, improving the opportunity offered by the absence of his hated rival, the adroit Nick Pappas showered time and attention and winning trivialities of a tangible sort upon the receptive daughter of Madame Renan.

Testifying to his ardor, and being in no small degree reassuring as to the nature of his intentions toward Mlle. Julie, there came a day when reiterated requests for "just a moment" with the Lieutenant procured for the black-haired Romeo the opportunity which he requested. "Lieutenant, the little girl and I have decided we want to get married," Nick announced after a preliminary skirmish. "You know, Lieutenant, you've got to have a birthday certificate signed and a superior officer O. K. your wedding."

"Fair enough. Who's the little girl?"

"Julie her name is—and maybe now that the reverend chaplain of the Regiment is boarding here in this camp you could make the order for him to say the wedding."

"All right, Nick—what else?"

"Maybe the Lieutenant would let me borrow the stylish Dodge automobile for a grand trip to Libourne on the honeymoon with a three-day pass."

"Sure I can—Chuck will haul you over there and come and get you. When are you going to get married?"

Now spoke the fox, seeking in his words to create a spectacular blow-off for his wedding which should include a final flight of the barbed arrows of jealousy, whose mark, when they found it, would be the absent Tex Miller. "Lieutenant, the little girl loves music, and we have decided not to get married until Mister Tex and his two music partners get back so maybe they can play at the wedding."

"You've got it all framed up, haven't you? All right,—let me know what to do and when to do it and I'll help you all I can."

The Gang, responding enthusiastically to the prospective bridegroom's invitation, inspired more by thoughts of a pleasurable diversion with free drinks furnished at somebody else's expense than by any fealty to their barbering blackjack associate, turned out in full force to help with the event.

Accompanied by the chaplain, the Loot

and several other officers of the company joined the Gang on Sunday morning and in a little while, escorting the bridegroom, the outfit descended in a body upon the Renan residence wherein the wedding ceremony was to be performed.

Tex, Rex and Mex, equipped with their several musical instruments, were welcomed by the bride's mother and then more effusively by Nick the Greek, who had already begun to assume an air of proprietorship over the Renan establishment. "You got competition," he announced to the trio. "We got a swell French orchestra for classic music."

"To hell with that stuff—where's the piano?"

Trying the piano, Rex found it more than equal to the occasion, and forthwith he launched into a ration of jazz while, surging about him, his companions in olive drab consumed copious supplies of liquid refreshment.

"Nix on that vang," some calm member of the Gang admonished, "and tell Rex for the love of this sacrificed dog-robber to lay off the jazz junk. Get him to play a funeral march or something before this joint is wrecked."

The calming influence of Tex Miller's violin and a moaning saxophone played by Mex succeeded in diverting the pianist to the more sedate items of his repertoire, and then, marshaling the contracting parties with a firmness befitting the occasion, the regimental chaplain began the text of the contract which bound together in wedded bliss until death or the duties of a dog-robber should part them, Nick the Greek and Mlle. Julie Renan.

Quickly then, Nick Pappas kissed his bride before any of the audacious Gang might beat him to it, but even as he embraced the girl he took occasion to flash a triumphant glance toward the defeated candidate for Julie's hand.

To his momentary annoyance he discovered no sign of distress upon Tex Miller's countenance.

Following this the bridegroom found himself the center of a clamorous group of Julie's relatives. Into the babble of felicitations drifted the soft music of the French orchestra which Madame Renan had provided for the event, but which, up to that time, had been backed off the boards by the livelier music played by the trio from the Gang.

At this interval, resting from his labors, Tex looked about him, seeking Madame Renan. His search was brief, for she was almost at his side, and the abruptness of his success in finding her smothered most of the complimentary phrases which he had formulated, leaving but one broken verbal tribute in the residue of his emotion. "Mon Dieu, cheery," he burst forth, "j'ai think vous est tray times more jolie than vou's petty enfant child."

"Merci, M'sieur Tex—and do you wish with me to taste one libation of champagne to the happiness of those pigeons?"

"Ah oui, mon cheery." At the moment, had Madame Louise elected to lead the way through a sea of champagne, Tex would have followed.

The pair withdrew to Madame Renan's dining room, where near a long buffet they discovered the chaplain and the Loot surrounded by a milling group of thirsty heroes.

Lifting her glass with a smile at her companion, Madame Renan seemed to have momentarily forgotten her interest in the welfare of her daughter and her daughter's new husband. "M'sieur Tex," she said softly, "I drink to you."

"Here's luck, mon tray dear cheery—drink hearty."

Madame Renan touched her lips to the wineglass and extended it to the blond giant beside her. "This we divide, as you say, 'fifty-fifty,'" the lady suggested, but something in her voice brought a sudden constriction to Tex's throat, and the distress of his pounding heart suffused his countenance.

He choked heroically, completing his conquest of obstinate vocal organs. He touched the hand of the lady beside him. "Fifty-fifty est tray bong . . . Louise, toujours fifty-fifty?"

Madame Renan closed her eyes for a brief moment, but even before she had opened them to reveal their message deep within, Tex had enlisted the Loot in his personal campaign. "We got the padre right here, Lieutenant—take a pencil and write me out a birth certificate like a man has got to have."

Without further urging the Loot did his part at record speed. The French orchestra in the adjoining room ceased playing. Tex reached out and accumulated one of the Gang. "Listen, Jugger," he ordered, "round up Isadog and give him my fiddle. Get Rex busy on that piano and tell Mex to fall in with a lungful of saxophone. Tell 'em to hit up 'Just A-wearyin' for You' and then to head into 'I Love You Truly,' and make it mighty soft."

"What's the big idea?"

"Do like I told you. Allay, soldier—we got to do right by Nick the Greek at a sentimental time like this, ain't we, no matter how we hate the louse? On your way."

In an adjoining room apart from the wedding guests, Tex and Madame Renan, escorted by the Loot, faced the chaplain of the Regiment and answered the chaplain's questions. "Absolute-mong! Yes!" Tex affirmed to one of these, with a vehemence which broke the soft refrain concerning life with its sorrows and life with its tears. "Ah oui—absolute-mong!"

After a few moments filled with appropriate sentiment Tex and his clinging vine, mingling with the guests in the Renan residence, encountered Nick the Greek. Lord now of all he surveyed, the latter permitted the affable Tex to express his hopes for the happiness of Nick's wedded career.

"Do not let that lay you awake nights, Tex," the Greek returned. "With the little Julie who is my bride comes plenty money—Madame Renan is a rich mamma. We will be happy enough, Tex. You should worry."

"Listen, Nick, git calm!" A red light blazed for an instant in Tex's smiling eyes. "You got a rich mamma, all right, you dog-robbin' gold digger,—but whenever you crave a issue of francs, come to papa. Git me? I'll toot your personal pay call. Me and your rich mamma is married. I and her have got to convoy some army mail to Paris for the

Loot, but when we get back if you ain't tamed down, you louse wino, your rich mamma is mighty apt to get herself a gold star to remember you by. Allay! You're in *my* army now!"

Chapter 5

BIGGER AND BETTER UPLIFT

WITH the first bright days of spring the Gang's domain was invaded by a crusading scourge of Uplifters. When this moral delousing plant had marched onward to bigger and better fields of sin, an example of human perfection was left on the warehouse job in the person of Alonzo Bluke. "I shall remain as sort of a sentinel—a shield interposed between your men and the temptations which throng about them," Alonzo explained to the Loot, seeking official recognition and moral support.

"Go to it—they're steeped in sin," the Loot assented. "Most of 'em need sentinels."

Following the plague of Uplifters had come what is known as a Series of Events.

Back in the U. S. A. the women prepared to vote, corset-makers turned their factories over to the manufacture of gas masks, and a famous soprano scored heavily with "Home, Sweet Home."

A detachment of telephone girls landed in war-torn France and arrangements were made whereby French war orphans could be taken care of for five hundred francs per year.

A prominent visiting fireman, making "a pilgrimage to the Temple of Heroism," enjoyed his "first contact with the actualities of war" in a Paris wine cellar. Orders issued making it imperative that the A. E. F. shave every other day.

The Distinguished Service Medal, garden seeds and Uplifters became part of the rewards and penalties of heroism; but neither telephone girls, shaves, war orphans, garden seeds, corset-makers nor votes for women bothered the Gang. Engaged in their own activities in the back yard of the Temple of Heroism, they let the rest of the world drift by until Alonzo Bluke dived into the scene.

Forthwith the Alonzo problem became acute.

Not content with laboring in his own local

vineyards in the U. S. A., striving to make his immediate vicinity a better place to live in, Alonzo the Uplifter had invaded the S. O. S. as soon as he discovered that the experience would be safe and pleasant with all expenses paid.

News of the Uplifter's arrival spread rapidly through the Gang's huts on the warehouse job. Alonzo had made a running start with his local reputation.

"Before I seen that he didn't have no backin'-up strap on his belt I dished out a salute, and what d'ya suppose the son-of-a-gun did?" a disgruntled member of the Gang announced.

"Probably asked you to help him carry something. That's what most of 'em do."

"A fat chance—do you know what he done? He took the salute like a jigadier brindle and come back with it before I seen he was a Uplifter. For two clackers I'd a crowned him. I thought they was a law against them birds comin' around here."

Spike Randall contributed a bit of information relative to Uplifters. "Law against 'em? Boy—it looks like there's an epidemic of 'em around this part of France. There must of been a shipload come across with those telephone girls. What did this bird look like?"

"Looked like an undertaker except for the leggin's he wore."

"You ain't got no kick comin' yet. The chances are he's on his way through this camp. We don't need no uplift. Ever since we been side-steppin' these next-door neighbors and coverin' a little more ground we been settin' pretty. Chuck and I went six miles past the furthest place they'd ever seen a M. P. last Sunday."

"Easy enough for you and Chuck to make the grade in that flivver of yours. Some guys has all the luck. Wish I could get transferred into your telephone crew about a week so I could see some country."

Enjoying peculiar advantages derived from the possession of a two-ton truck and a flivver, Spike Randall and his telephone detail had managed to explore a zone far beyond the pedestrian limit where in a side line of duty they had uncovered many of the hidden delights of the more distant reaches of their environment.

Little villages and inns where they were welcomed, private residences where they could eat hearty, drink in peace, and enjoy the companionship of affable French people, served to make a job with Spike and his telephone gang a capital prize in the military lottery.

At first the telephone detail had been careful to guard its pleasant sanctuaries and to keep them well under cover; but friendship is friendship, and in a little while Patsy and Fat and Mike and twenty more charter members of the Gang were welcome visitors in fifty places off the beaten path between Bordeaux and Libourne.

Seven miles south of the warehouse project was the village of Arborsac. The little hamlet was undistinguished from other settlements which drowsed apart from the alarms of war, save that its population included Cleopatra, red-headed queen of village queens. By the Gang's unanimous vote, in a field of beauties who had charmed the brave and loving Soldats Américains, Cleopatra was a three-time winner.

She of the flaming hair, born in Algiers, lived on the edge of Arborsac in an old stone house where, with her husband's mother, she waited in vain for her man's returning because he was too pleasantly employed in Paris.

Behind her house was a little inclosure of ground on a southern slope, and here were vines planted, from whose grapes wines of rare flavor had been pressed; and on another patch of ground bordering the shade of three ancient trees there was a patch of strawberries whose juices matched Cleopatra's hair.

Without being dangerous, something about the Algerian girl suggested danger, and that may have been her attraction for the hardened veterans in the Gang who had been everywhere and had seen everything.

Wine and strawberries, a free afternoon, sunshine that meant something—"Hot dam, soldier, home was never like this!"

Then, when the local paradise had begun to

Bigger and Better Uplift 149

live up to specifications, prowling into the scene came the invading Uplifter.

For a while the human soul seemed to be his objective, and then he began to promote jolly athletic meets.

"Jimmy the Ink has got a new dish for you rabble," the Top confided to the Gang after supper had been salvaged and before the evening's activities had claimed free members of the Gang. "It came in the afternoon mail. The Loot said to post it on the board and to hell with it. You birds better read it and see what you're up against."

An inspection of the bulletin board disclosed the fact that Alonzo Bluke would forthwith consecrate himself to the physical welfare of all troops in the camp. "He sure come loaded. That order is got the O. K. of the Base Commander on it."

"Boy, that's what we need—bokoo physical welfare. Juggle ourselves a flock of warehouses all day long and see how fast you can make a hundred-yard dash when Alonzo shoots the gun after supper."

"That louse better look some place else for

customers. Personally I wouldn't wish no more physical culture than I get fightin' that damn Belgian bullgine all day long. That muscle maniac is going to be just as popular as that dope they put in the drinking water at Genimont,—and he pains me the same way."

"Maybe all he aims to do is take care of these idle tourists that drift through here—most of those outfits don't do nothing but lay around camp all day, anyhow."

Old Pop Sibley contributed a philosophical comment on the problem. "You boys take it easy," he advised. "If wust comes to wust, the Loot kin hang him or a grivance committee could take it up with General Pershing. The chances are he don't aim to pester us hired hands none."

Alas for prophecy. In the S. O. S. the best laid plans had a habit of going wrong. "Finish Warehouse 38 by Friday night," the Loot had announced, "and as far as I'm concerned you can have Saturday and Sunday all your own." Then, making the holiday more worth while: "Spike is in the clear on that Libourne wire, and maybe he'll detail

Bigger and Better Uplift 151

Chuck and the two-ton truck to haul you wherever you want to go. Rig it up any way you want, but you'd better keep away from the bright lights."

Midway of their plans for a two-day ruckus, "Everything's busted sideways," Red Walker announced, coming into the Gang's hut with news of an impending disaster. "Blowed high, wide an' handsome! The Uplifter is pulling an athletic meet. Busts up that artillery ball game, ruins them stevedore boys' minstrel show, knocks the passes all to hell and gums our own game from soup to sinkers. Everybody turns out Saturday afternoon for a workout, the order says, and then Sunday everybody rallies for a mess of running and jumping and junk like that."

"I'm too durned old to run and jump," Pop Sibley protested when the silence had become ominous.

"You ain't too old to cheer for the winner —nobody gets loose. Whoever side-steps the spotlight in Alonzo's game has got to stick close alongside to help with the cheering."

An informal investigation committee, seeking the Loot's counsel, found nothing to comfort them. "Orders is orders," the Loot set forth. "This bird has got us tied in a sack with his hand-picked holiday. We've got to draw cards and sit into the game whether we like it or not. I might make a play for two or three squads, but the Alonzo bird has got the whole company roped and there she lays."

Assembling to discuss the thing, "It's just like the Loot says," one of the Gang affirmed. "He can't kidnap the company and he don't want to play no favorites. We're up against this thing—let's go through with it."

Forthwith, having resolved to go through with whatever Uplifter Alonzo Bluke might have in store for them, a dozen members of the Gang devoted themselves to formulating some scheme whereby this first general atrocity perpetrated by Alonzo Bluke might mark the end of his activities.

Late that night Isadog and Jugger, wrestling with the problem, struck the first stringer that later led the Gang to a pay streak of rich revenge. "Get Spike outside here till we tell it to him," Isadog directed. "We can't do nothing unless he sees it our way. You dead sure about that new M. P. detachment?"

Jugger spoke with undue harshness. "Listen, Isadog, you infidel skeptic, I told you once me and this Buck Hammer that's sergeant of the M. P. detail worked a claim together in Placer County all one summer. While Buck's runnin' them M. P.'s they're just like we owned 'em. Go on and round up Spike and I'll meet you at the café at Vayres."

Half an hour later, apart from the rest of the world in the back room of the little inn on the river bank at Vayres, Spike and Isadog met the waiting Jugger. An unusual enthusiasm marked the latter's mood, while Isadog, more given to exhibiting his varying temperament, held himself under control only by exercising deliberate efforts to that end.

"Listen, Spike," he said excitedly as the parley began, "we got this Alonzo Bluke man standing with one foot on a banana peel and the other touching a trolley wire. You lend us Chuck and your two-ton truck, and by

Monday morning that file closer in Mister Uplifter's army won't be nothing but a gap in the ranks. Listen while I tell you what Jugger and I got framed. . . ."

News of the forthcoming field day spread rapidly through the various organizations engaged on the warehouse project, and in a little while the event promised to gratify Alonzo Bluke's wildest ambitions.

"The enthusiasm of the men is quite touching," he wrote to a brother Uplifter back in the United States. "The track meet and general jollification which I am arranging for the boys around here next Sunday promises to be quite popular. It is very gratifying to see the way the flower of Democracy shuns the local temptations whenever opportunity for good, clean sport is vouchsafed unto them. I have wrestled with my conscience about the matter of indulging in sports on the Sabbath, but a still small voice within me seems to say that it is well that the hills and dales of this fair land should become a temple wherein our soldier boys might approach a little nearer to spiritual beauties while resting from their labors."

While Alonzo was wrestling with his conscience concerning the Sunday fiesta, that event, enjoying a normal increment of publicity from the current gossip related beyond the confines of the warehouse project, enlisted to its support half of the local French population. On Saturday when the tryouts for the various events were being staged the camp was thronged with spectators interested in the sport of the Americans.

The innocent bystanders included representatives of both sexes, and this immediately imposed a problem relative to suitable athletic raiment. The problem was finally solved by a genius who suggested the lower half of a B. V. D. equipment appropriately altered by means of a needle and thread. "A man can't run and jump in his uniform, and them denim overalls clutters his legs all up. That flannel underwear is no good. Only thing to do is to sew up a pair of B. V. D. drawers."

"Ain't we goin' to wear no shirts?"

"Sure we're goin' to wear shirts. They got to paint numbers on 'em for one thing to tell who you are, and for another thing the flies around camp since we got so many visitors would eat you up."

The various outfits in the camp contributed large detachments of ambitious applicants for the preliminary tryouts. When it developed that the athletic talent in the Gang included no one capable of shining in any of the events save the three-mile run, the Uplifter graciously permitted the Gang to assume a private title to this part of the affair.

"This three-mile cross-country run will be your very own celebration," Alonzo announced to the Gang. "But remember, fellows, if you are not used to continued exertion it will be a trying affair for you. I trained for the mile at the Seminary for months and months before our physical instructor let me try the longer distances. . . . Of course, leading you as I shall, I will be enabled to hold the pace down to something not too strenuous. Remember—we are not trying to break any records. We are going into this only for the glorious exhilaration that comes when mind and body are perfectly attuned."

While all of this mush was being ladled out to the Gang by the uplifting Alonzo, Spike Randall exchanged the compliments of the season and other friendly sentiments with Sergeant Kinsey of the negro labor battalion, whose efforts were just then contributing so largely to the construction program of the storage depot.

Sergeant Kinsey, one of the best soldiers in the A. E. F., listened with attentive ear. When Spike had outlined his requirements a broad smile of understanding spread over the black man's honest face.

"Six or eight of your men will be enough," Spike concluded, "but the main thing will be to pick a crew out of your outfit who can jabber in French."

"Dat comes mighty easy to some of dese niggers," Sergeant Kinsey returned. "Mighty lot of 'em comes f'm Loosiana an' is already agile wid dis French talk."

A little while later, to a selected group of his protégés in the labor battalion, "Lissen at me whilst you gits commanded!" the black and burly Sergeant Kinsey ordered. Forthwith, in accordance to Spike Randall's specifications, a program covering the immediate future was communicated to the detail in a strictly military manner.

"'Filiate wid dem French niggers some place to-night an' 'range fo' yo' raiment," Sergeant Kinsey advised his flock. "Dat's all I got to tell you 'cept one thing—does ennybody make enny mistakes, de nex' bugle music whut he hears is gwine to be played by de Angel Gabriel on his resurrecktin' horn. . . . Detail—'tenshun! Dis-misted!"

While the blackface detail was getting its orders Spike Randall, following his conversation with Sergeant Kinsey, had made a quick exit toward Arborsac in the telephone crew's flivver.

Arrived at the village, he went directly to an inn where, lingering over a glass of beer, he exchanged a few items of gossip with half a dozen villagers. Had the peaceful town of Arborsac been molested by any chance by any

Bigger and Better Uplift 159

of the escaped patients from the Americans' insane hospital?

Up to date it appeared that Arborsac had been spared.

That was indeed fortunate, but with the epidemic of insanity which had suddenly afflicted some of the homesick troops, in Spike's opinion, vigilance was the price of safety. Alas for the dread by-products of the conflict! Escaped prisoners, escaped crazy men—the land had indeed fallen into evil days. . . . But with the brave Sergeant Hammer of the Military Police Arborsac indeed had little to fear. Did anyone present by any chance know the whereabouts of Sergeant Hammer at the moment?

Five eager informants volunteered information to the effect that at the moment Sergeant Hammer could no doubt be found in the house of the red-haired Algerian girl, enjoying strawberries and wine.

With that, stressing his limited vocabulary within an inch of its life, Spike managed to convey his sorrow at the necessity for his early departure. He climbed into the flivver and retraced his route until at the edge of Arborsac he stopped in front of the house wherein, with her mother, lived the red-haired Cleopatra.

After appropriate and heartfelt greetings had been exchanged, Spike inquired for the M. P. sergeant.

"Under the tree in the back garden the Sergeant Hammer is sitting, enjoying a glass of wine with his strawberries. Will you not join him?"

The answer was yes.

"Everything is all set for Sunday," Spike informed the congenial M. P. "The local stuff will keep everybody busy until somewhere around four o'clock in the afternoon, and then the Alonzo Uplifter figures on pulling the trigger on his three-mile run. For the love of the double-jointed dog-robber don't miss your play when the cards drop for the big deal."

"I'll be Johnny-at-the-rat-hole with a short fuse lighted, old-timer," Sergeant Buck Hammer returned. "Give my regards to the

Jugger when you see him and tell the pack rat to hunt me up."

"I will . . . and listen, Buck, if we pull this drag under the wire on schedule, the Gang won't never forget how much they owe you."

"They don't owe me nothin'—I'm with 'em in the play from the starting gun till when the firin' squad shoots an echo. So long."

The pair shook hands, and in his flivver Spike Randall returned to camp, where he reported at once to Isadog and Jugger.

"Everything's all set for the big play at Arborsac," he assured his fellow conspirators. "Is the Loot ridin' with us?"

"You bet your last clacker he is. The Loot's in this play up to his neck. That's one reason why nothin' can't go wrong. If anything slips they might soak us ninety days at the outside, but they'd bust him."

"Not without lots of company—and you know what company I mean."

"Sure I do. Git to sleep, you blackhander —hit the hay. You'll need bokoo pep for the physical culture Alonzo aims to boon you with to-morrow."

The physical culture round-up promoted by Alonzo Bluke was staged on a level field four miles south of the warehouse project. To this point rallied spectators and participants from the construction forces engaged on the work and from a dozen near-by settlements.

Spontaneous crops of peddlers mingled with the throng, children got lost, the retail trade in romance reached a new level, and the high laughter of negro stevedores rang above their fellows' entreaties of encouragement directed toward somnolent sevens on galloping dominoes.

In and out of the scene, seemingly prominent at all four points of the compass, buzzed Alonzo Bluke. Cheering the winners, burbling heartfelt sympathy to the losers, Alonzo absorbed the spotlight, running the show until, fed up on frenzy, three-fourths of the spectators and nearly all of the participants had retired to engage in pleasanter occupations.

At four o'clock in the afternoon when the three-mile run was scheduled the gallery had dwindled to a few French people and a contingent of colored casualties who had lost their individual battles with old Demon Rum.

"Ladies and gentlemen," Alonzo announced, "the final event will be the three-mile run, and this will conclude the day's festivities. In this event I will participate personally." To the Gang, grouped beside the telephone crew's two-ton truck on the seat of which sat Spike and Chuck, "All ready, fellows, for the cross-country run!"

Alonzo began to divest himself of his raiment. Off came his leather belt and his blouse and presently, continuing his disrobing process, Alonzo stood forth in a cotton union suit which at once afforded leg action and an appropriate screen of modesty between Alonzo's anatomy and a gaping world.

"Fall in and march past the artist!"

"Git your numbers painted on you."

"Git branded, slaves."

In single file, after hats and shirts, overalls and shoes had been stowed in the two-ton truck, the Gang marched past Old Pop Sibley, who, wielding a paint brush, branded the backs of their undershirts with winning numbers.

"Save that thirteen for Isadog."

"Give me a 7–11, Pop."

"Stick a 23 on me. I aim to go some."

Playing the game and radiating sweetness, Alonzo the Uplifter took his place in the line.

"Aw, don't paint Mister Bluke's shirt. Don't spoil his underwear."

"Yes, indeed, fellows," Alonzo protested. "I am one of you—I insist."

In a loud voice up spoke Isadog. "Mister Bluke ain't one of us common rabble. He's a participating guest. Give him something special."

"I kain't spell 'participating.'" Old Pop Sibley paused with his dripping brush arrested in its dive toward Alonzo's back.

"P. G. stands for participating guest—

paint P. G. on Mister Bluke, and let it go at that."

"That will do nicely." Alonzo smiled his approval and submitted to the branding process, writhing slightly under the sting of the turpentine in the thin paint. The Uplifter took his place in the line and waited for the gun.

"All ready, Loot—let 'er go!" Nervous impatience marked the speaker's words as the Loot limbered up a .45.

Bang! Paced by Alonzo Bluke, the field strung out in its three-mile gallop toward Arborsac. When the runners were half a mile away Spike, on the front seat of the two-ton truck, nodded to Chuck. "Let's go," he said. "Take it easy. We don't want to run 'em down."

For the favored spectators clustered around the arena, Alonzo put on a burst of speed as a farewell exhibition of his ability and then, leading the field, he disappeared over the brow of a low hill.

Keen-eyed observers noted that on the up grade leading to the summit of the next hill

Alonzo was leading all competitors by several hundred yards. Then around a curve in the road the Uplifter and his straggling followers passed onward in their flight toward the good, the true, the beautiful.

When half of the race had been run, still holding himself down to a gait which he figured was well within the powers of the Gang to emulate, Alonzo looked back along a hundred-yard stretch of the course in an effort to observe the status of his competitors, but none of the Gang was in sight. For a moment the Uplifter contemplated slackening his pace until the lagging runners could come up with him, but abruptly he changed his mind.

His attention was suddenly attracted by a wild burst of threatening language which came from an excited group of Senegalese negroes clad in the cloth of those savage French Colonials.

From where they had been lounging in the shade of a roadside tree half a dozen excited blacks leaped toward Alonzo, and something in their manner conveyed to him the thought of danger. Some sinister menace marked the actions of the Senegalese!

Alonzo shifted to high.

A second later, when three of the group quartered toward him at a gallop, his foreboding was confirmed because, flashing in the swinging arms of the leading negro there gleamed the long blade of a knife.

Alonzo remembered current rumors conveying the characteristics of the fighters who threatened him. Enthusiastic addicts of the bayonet! Notably averse to hampering their activities with prisoners! Killers and fanatics in their bloodthirsty devotion to cold steel!

Alonzo craved solitude, but solitude seemed mighty scarce. Escape was cut off. The clutching hand of the leading Senegalese closed on a clammy fold of the Uplifter's costume.

A babble of guttural French lifted from the panting ring of perspiring assassins about Alonzo while, shuddering until his protruding kneecaps clattered in cadence with his chattering teeth, he culled his vocabulary in search of a prayer in Senegalese.

The knife in the hand of the violent African made a quick slash through the upper section of Alonzo's raiment. A second later, on the shredded section of the union suit worn by the Participating Guest Alonzo read the mute evidence which had inspired the frantic Senegalese to this enjoyable atrocity. "P. G."—not "Participating Guest" but, as the leader of the Senegalese growled in his rage, "Prisonnier de Guerre! Boche!"

"Mort au Boche!"

"Mort, mort"—the word had a familiar sound. . . . Sure enough, Mort was the equal of sudden death. . . .

Sunny France turned black for an instant in Alonzo's eyes. His brain reeled under the impact of the babble about him; and then toward one narrow avenue of escape, galvanized by fear, the Uplifter leaped in a kangaroo jump that gave him a twenty-foot lead on the murderous Senegalese.

Parting from his captors he left another ripping section of his costume in their leader's grasp, but what were details at a time like this? Onward he sped away from his brutal, bellowing pursuers until, nearing the sanctuary of Arborsac, he realized that he had been spared miraculously for further labors in the Vineyard.

Behind him, after a false start, the Senegalese sidetracked in a body and halted under a roadside tree where, removing their outer raiment, they stood revealed as members of the stevedore battalion from the warehouse.

"Dat boy sho' done noble wid dem hind laigs of hisn," one of the panting participants in the little drama exulted, storing his Senegalese raiment into a canvas sack which had been brought along to serve as a wardrobe chest.

"Seems like us done middlin' noble, too, big boy," one of his companions returned. "Ol' Sergeant Kinsey gwine to be mighty pleased wid de way his li'l Senegalese niggers won de battle wid dat white boy. Chances is he boons you wid a Bo'deaux pass wheneveh you craves it f'm now on. Tie up dat sack—heah comes de truck."

A more immediate reward fell to the faithful stevedore detachment when, after reporting their progress and their success to Spike Randall, seated beside Chuck on the two-ton truck, a shower of francs fell in their midst out of the hands of a dozen members of the Gang who were housed in the canvas cover above the bed of the vehicle.

Answering Isadog's inquiry, "Yas suh, dat white boy kep' runnin'," one of the Senegalese replied.

"Does he keep goin' like he started, he gwine to be in Memphis by midnight," another one added.

"Fair enough. The rest of the play is up to Cleopatra and Buck Hammer," another member of the Gang observed. "Let's get the hell out of here and get an alibi built up. Step on 'er, Chuck!"

Leaving the route of the three-mile run, riding the two-ton truck driven by Chuck, the runners in the race busied themselves with the business of dressing en route to Libourne and its pleasing pastures of recuperation where the fatigue of a false start could be eradicated from the human system by judicious internal applications of various beverages.

The Gang, withdrawn in a body from the cross-country race, abandoned pursuit of the galloping Alonzo, but following that athlete's escape from the savage Senegalese it seemed that old man Trouble sprained a wrist in dealing Alonzo another card from the stacked deck of Fate.

Human habitations, civilization, sanctuary from peril—Arborsac meant this to the flying Alonzo. To dive into the first friendly house he came to, there to engage the sympathy of some French Samaritan—sweet was the contemplated nectar of safety!

Alonzo checked his course abruptly at the open door of the first house he came to. He dived in. "Bonjour!" he said weakly, directing his salutation into the silent house.

A wild scream answered him, and this first alarm was echoed by a succession of wilder screams which burst from the parted lips of a frantic young woman with red hair and robust lungs.

Alonzo glanced down at the remaining fragments of his costume. "My dear Madame—" he began. His words seemed to have calmed the startled Cleopatra, but this was a false hope, for the red-haired one burst forth with a new emotion which found expression in convulsive sobs.

"Mon Dieu, mon cheery!" Alonzo continued, extending his hand toward the frantic girl in an effort to calm her. "Mon——"

"What the hell!" A deep bass voice interrupted the scene and against the light of the open doorway behind him Alonzo the Uplifter saw the silhouette of Sergeant Buck Hammer. "What's goin' on here!"

The calloused hand of Sergeant Hammer closed around the Uplifter's neck.

"Mon Dieu!" the captive gasped. "Do you parley English?"

"Come along, wild man—the judge will parley bokoo English for you. Shut up before I sap you! Runnin' around naked, breakin' into ladies' houses—shut up! Don't answer me back. . . ."

Sergeant Buck Hammer marched his pris-

Bigger and Better Uplift 173

oner out of the house and along the main street of Arborsac to the central square of the town. A group of chattering villagers had accumulated along the route. "Is it true that the Sergeant has captured a crazy man?"

"Of a certainty—regard, if you please, the abbreviated costume which none but a crazy man wears."

"That is possible; but alas, could not this shameless man have been surprised at some rendezvous with a lady, so to speak?"

Ah, yes, such might indeed be the case!

"Let us, then, fling a bombardment of mud at this animal."

By no means—the brave Sergeant of the Military Police would arrange all details of the execution.

Sergeant Buck Hammer indeed had the situation well in hand. "Ravin' about this and that and the other thing," he reported to his relief at six o'clock. "I'm gonna take him to Bordeaux in the side car and lock him up before he gets any worse. He's good for twenty years in jail, as near as I can see—that is if he misses the firin' squad."

Cut to the cold details of circumstantial evidence, the Sergeant's report covering the last chapter of the Uplifter's activities inspired a brief command from heavyweight military authority. "More to be pitied than censured, no doubt—but request his dismissal through the proper authorities of his organization and ship him to the United States. 'Temperamentally unfit.'—Too damn many of 'em buzzing around here, anyhow."

Some days later, along with the evening mail, a courier from Bordeaux relayed an item of information to the Gang. "One of them field clerks down at Headquarters told me your Uplifter athlete got the skids put under him."

Gazing sadly at the courier over the steel rim of his spectacles, Old Pop Sibley answered for the Gang. "Sonny," he said, "Alonzo is gone but not forgotten. He aimed noble to uplift us, but mebbe his last ca'tridge missed fire. Leave us groan our woe, Rabble, f'r his like will ne'er be seen again."

Chapter 6

Fifteen Hundred Bucks

BLACK WEEK hit the Gang after a monotonous string of days and nights filled with plain hard work. A rumor relative to pay day inspired long thoughts of vang, vimmen and vocal exercises.

In spite of deductions the blackjack financiers and dice addicts were in a gloatful mood, for Lady Luck had booned the Gang with an increment of ten Replacements whose travels had kept them one jump ahead of the Pay Call for six months.

"Figger it out for yourself," Jimmy the Ink advised. "These ten birds drag down over thirty dollars a month, and that's three hundred dollars. They ain't heard the pay car rumble for five months. That adds up to a Grand and a half."

"Fifteen hundred bucks!"

"Us Rabble can reap bokoo profits if the cards drop right."

"They'll drop right—no stranger ever had a chance in this outfit."

Contemplated profits to accrue from the Replacement victims gave rise to a train of engagements scheduled to follow the last notes of the Pay Call. "Lissen, mon cheery, bokoo francs will be put out probably right after supper. I git me a mess of poker or blackjack or craps, and then toot sweet me and vous promenade to Bordeaux in a hack. That sounds tray bean, nest pa?"

Of a surety the prospectus glittered. "And when is it to be the pay day?"

"Probably when the Loot gets back from Bordeaux Saturday afternoon."

Returning from Bordeaux on Saturday afternoon, the Loot brought with him an intangible cargo of shattered hopes. "No pay until next week." In the Dodge at the Loot's right sat a sour major, wearing whiskers. "Major Pedicure will orate a lecture on the care of the feet immediately after supper," the Loot announced at Retreat.

Fifteen Hundred Bucks 177

Morale evaporated into the steam that floated above the potato kettle when Mess Call blew. In return for an oversized ration of goldfish Old Pop Sibley promulgated a theme to which, presently, all of the old-timers in the Gang added their venomous contributions. "Looks like A. E. F. means 'All Eat Fish,'" Pop Sibley grumbled. "I'm fed up on fins. The feller that wrote Columbia the Gem of the Ocean prolly meant the Columbia River, where salmon is thickest."

"Ever since we went to work for Uncle Sam we been eatin' Uncle Salmon. Rabble, there's a trick in it some place."

After supper, adding insult to injury, Major Pedicure held forth on The Care of the Feet.

"What us damn heroes need is somebody to orate on The Care of the Stomach instead of our damn feet."

"Yeah—you sure got plenty of feet."

"Boy, these shoes ain't my size. I can do a right-face inside these shoes without movin' 'em. They's so much room in these shoes that when I walked to work this morning they didn't get there till five minutes after I did."

"Shut up. Whiskers is goin' to begin his show."

"A soldier cannot march with sore feet," Major Pedicure began, and then, drooling through the rest of the quotation from the Manual, he added a burbling hour laden with four-cylinder words and technical phrases which left the Gang ready for whatever desperate enterprise might offer temporary relief.

After Taps, in a heart-to-heart conference with the Loot, "Something's got to break around here pretty soon or something's gonna bust," the Top predicted.

"Something will break," the Loot affirmed, voicing his faith in Lady Luck. "There's nothing seriously wrong with the Gang as long as they say it out loud. Safety valve. We don't have to worry until the Gang begins to bottle up its bellyaches. The ration question is——"

The Loot was interrupted by the roar of a motorcycle which halted with a volley of exhausts at the door of the Headquarters shack.

Fifteen Hundred Bucks   179

In the wake of an orderly a courier came tramping down the hallway.

"Lieutenant, here's a hot note from the Colonel," the courier announced, discarding all of his military manner. Then, to eliminate suspense, "The Regiment is ordered to the front!"

Three paragraphs into the formal order, the Loot was deaf to outside things. He nodded absently to the courier's announcement.

Speaking quietly to the orderly who fidgeted in the doorway, anticipating a preliminary to the impending activity, "Wake up Squad One and tell 'em to report here right now," Spike Randall ordered.

Quietly the Loot read through the seven paragraphs of the order which meant Action, and then, to Spike, "The Regiment assembles and moves up in three drags. Get me some messengers . . . we get transportation at 5 A.M. Highball at six." The Loot scribbled five names on a sheet of note paper and handed it to the Top. "Send a man out pronto with a flock of compliments and get these officers in here on the run. They take charge of the project when we leave. Break out the rifles and some portable chow. Get the lieutenants on deck. Round up any of the Gang that are on night shift. Tell Frog to get on the switchboard and keep a line cleared to the Base and another to Regimental Headquarters, wherever the hell that is. The company will assemble, all dolled up, at midnight."

While the Lieutenant was speaking, the Top, impelled by some long-abandoned instinct, got up from the chair in which he had slouched in a comfortable position, and stood at attention.

The act was an index of the transition which that night characterized the morale of the Gang.

At midnight, facing the company, the Loot was conscious of the fact that the outfit had clicked into an intelligent submission to military discipline. Easy and informal things had vanished, and here, where construction men had drooped at ease, was a fighting unit, rigid at attention.

Fifteen Hundred Bucks 181

A new respect, an increment of admiration for his outfit, filled the heart of the Lieutenant as the Gang barked their responses to the roll call through the darkness. They were on the eve of realizing the great ambition which had swept them into the Big Game. It seemed as if the old chagrin which the Gang had felt when its prompt answer to the nation's first appeal had gone unheeded was swept away by this acknowledgment of its country's need. High Command had at last confessed its dependence on the Gang, and eagerly, into the black night, the Gang responded.

"Corporal Badger."

Silence. Corporal Badger, A. W. O. L., was in a fair way to get himself ventilated by a firing squad.

And then, before three seconds of silence had punctuated the roll call, from his position ten paces behind Jimmy the Ink, the Loot barked, "Here!"

The Gang took a deep breath—"The Loot can figure it out some way—" and returned to its long, long thoughts. Plenty of cartridges.

Without 'em this gun is a ten-pound nuisance . . . damn these new shoes . . . eight suits of underwear is too much for a man to wear . . . I bet Fifi will miss me—and the Lord make mine a bullet or a lump of shell . . . the bayonet. Thrust, lunge, strike, cut . . . even if you get stuck clean through your guts there's a little dingus inside you that squirts sort of a pain-killer into your blood and you don't feel it . . . don't feel it much. . . . Well, whichever way she breaks is all right with me. That's what I come for . . .

At half-past five, in a drizzle of rain, the Gang climbed into the long train which was to haul it up the line.

Ten minutes before the hour scheduled for their departure, the police detail, having conquered its mountains of abandoned débris, came up, was checked on board, and stowed itself away in the cramped freight cars. Acute discomforts were regarded lightly or neglected, for here was the beginning of the Real Thing.

At five minutes to six another company of the Regiment, jerked from its own job and assembled as a fighting unit, came rolling in on its special train which stood abreast of the Gang's rolling stock on the main line. A din of salutations echoed back and forth between the two trains. Everybody knew everybody, and no rain could dampen the Gang's delight.

Three minutes before the hour, accompanied by the Chef de Gare, the Loot and the Top came out of the railway station and headed for the train on the side track. Midway of the train the Chef de Gare essayed an overture on the penny whistle which should presently launch the Gang into the great adventure. The ridiculous quality of the penny whistle piping went unnoticed; then, realizing the significance of this signal, the Gang submerged the thin, shrill notes in a cheer whose answer roared back with equal enthusiasm from their companion company on the main line.

The Chef de Gare consulted briefly with the engine men standing beside the locomotive on the head end of the Gang's train. "And then, M'sieur, if you please, at precisely the sixth hour you will make the movement of this train."

"Of a certainty, M'sieur." That was the program, and the program should suffer fulfillment within one little minute.

The Chef de Gare expressed his gratification by playing a shrill encore on his penny whistle.

Midway of the piece a telephone operator galloped out of Headquarters office. He ran toward the head of the Gang's train, and as he ran, testifying to his haste, he clawed a head-set from his ears and yelled a message loudly enough for all the Gang to hear:

"Hold the deal! You got new orders!"

A sledge hammer of gloom hit every man who heard the cry. The rain became real rain. Hurrying ahead alongside the train to encounter the messenger, the Loot's heart sank. Any orders at this moment would be an unwelcome negative to the program of perfection. Nearing the messenger, "What's the deal?" the Loot yelled.

"Base Headquarters says hold the train," the panting switchboard man returned.

"Last night's orders is canceled. My pardner is receiving some new dope for your outfit over the phone."

After a moment's quick conversation with the Chef de Gare and the engine man, the Loot retraced his steps toward the telephone office where the operator was just then recording the final paragraph of an order which slammed the Gang and the Regiment back to the prosaic labor of its lately abandoned construction work.

Presently, three hells deeper than the lowest level of human despair, the Gang assembled in a company front beside its old quarters.

The Loot estimated his problem and spoke with brevity: "All-night passes will be issued for those who want them. Blow back here sometime—if it is convenient." He turned the Company over to the Top and retreated rapidly toward Headquarters hut.

A sackful of official mail had arrived, and Jimmy the Ink was attacking it with a butcher knife. The Loot glanced wearily at the accumulating stack of communications which had filtered out of the great reservoir of the A. E. F. through military channels to his desk. He looked at the uppermost letter:

> "A recent investigation discloses the fact that you have made no use of consignment of garden seeds shipped to you from this office on the 3rd inst. In view of the crucial status of foodstuffs for the A. E. F. you will at once explain what disposition was made of seed peas and beans sent to you, and if culpable negligence is indicated, appropriate action of utmost severity will be taken."

The Loot recalled the savory soup which had been created out of the garden seeds. He dropped the letter into the wastebasket beside the desk.

"Never mind the mail," he said to Jimmy the Ink. "Let it ride for a while. Please get on the telephone and get me the Chapeau Rouge." While the call was being put through the Loot reached for his pocketbook and opened it. He audited the stack of bank notes and gazed deeply into the future.

"Here's the boss of the restaurant," Jimmy

the Ink announced, handing the telephone to the Loot.

"I will be in for dinner to-night after the show is over at the Apollo Theater," the Loot informed the proprietor of the Chapeau Rouge.

The establishment would be honored. "Accompanied by guests of what number?"

"Ten, perhaps twenty—how many ladies are in the chorus of the Apollo?"

"I should estimate that there are perhaps forty in the ensemble."

"Fair enough. Half of 'em will have idle hours to while away. My dear old devil, you would better prepare for, let us say, a party of thirty."

"A thrice admirable arrangement. Give no thought to the details."

Forgetting the details, the Lieutenant hung up. "If Chuck is lurking around with the Dodge, tell him I would like to go to Bordeaux," he said to Jimmy the Ink. "You can lock up the records and ride down with me if you care to start your own holiday. And listen, Jimmy, something tells me that I'm to be Queen of the May, so if I don't show up here by Tuesday, maybe you and Slim and Blackie and Jugger and some more of the old-timers better hop into Bordeaux and accumulate the quivering remains."

"Loot, you ain't runnin' wild again, are you, after bein' tame for nearly a year?"

"Boy, what you don't know is largely due to your ignorance. See if you can find Chuck and that rubber-tired Dodge hack."

In spite of Sabbath calm, when the Loot reached Bordeaux that city was neither calm nor peaceful. Through its streets, seeking diversion, prowled some thousands of soldiers enjoying Sunday passes.

Arriving at the Restaurant Gruber, the Loot bought three cheering drinks for himself, his passengers and Chuck, after which he endowed the latter with whatever liberty adroit members of the Gang might enjoy in the local environment. "Park the Dodge around the corner and run wild as long as you crave to," he said to Chuck. "I'll drive it back to camp to-morrow or the day after or maybe later than that."

Alone now at the marble-topped table in the alcove to the right of the entrance to the establishment, the Loot contemplated the day that had passed. His reverie was interrupted by a quiet interrogation from his waiter, a veteran of Verdun. "The hand of Fate has then, perhaps, dealt you a blow of some severity?"

"It has—but I had no idea that the advertising was so lurid. You will pardon me, Alexander, for wearing my personal troubles inside out." The Loot looked at the spot where part of Alexander's jaw had been shot away, and at the veteran's left eye, which was blind, and was ashamed of himself.

"The day will brighten. In distress the present hour is forever darkest . . . an encore of the apéritif?"

"No more, thank you. I'm going out for a walk in the sunlight."

After ten minutes in the open air, warmed by the rare sunlight which flooded Bordeaux, the Loot realized that, more than anything else, he needed a sympathetic listener. He scanned the assemblage seated at the little round tables fronting the Café Bordeaux, hoping that he might discover in the throng some congenial acquaintance. He was about to turn away, disappointed, when an American officer addressed him. "Lieutenant, won't you join me?" The speaker, seated alone at a table, got to his feet and held out his hand. "I'm Jim Rocca, the dago date grower from Indio, California. Quartermaster. Merely a quartermaster—a little stranger pining for his southern home in dear old Indio."

After the fourth cocktail, "Wonder what makes the ice so hot in this damn place?" the quartermaster captain complained.

"Come with me," the Loot invited. "They have the coolest ice in the world at Gruber's. My old friend Alexander will shake up an arctic expedition that will freeze your eskimos. After that you will have lunch with me?"

"With bokoo gusto. Lead on—I'm only a visiting fireman around here."

Leaving the scene, Captain Rocca overlooked a low step and demolished four tables and the Sabbath calm in his transit of the sidewalk.

The Loot assisted his companion to his feet. "Steady, you old Rock of Gibraltar. Remember the special confidence paragraph in your commission."

"Trivial. A mere trophy. I mean a mere truffle. Trifle. Hogs root truffles up with their noses."

"Come on, Avalanche. The ice fields you craved lie north by east."

"Sailor?"

"Engineer."

"Same thing. I thought them two castles was forecastles. I'm a rare wit, and damn me for a Gila monster but I'm glad I met you! I got troubles I got to tell you."

The Loot remembered something about his own troubles. "So've I. We'll put in the afternoon telling troubles."

"Get 'em all told, then go lookin' for some more. What's your trouble?"

"Heroism. I love my native land."

"So do I—but my trouble is, I love too many of its lady citizens. That's one of my troubles. That's the reason I came over here. Right now my main trouble is finance."

"Don't worry, boy." The Loot reached for his hip pocket. "I got me two or three thousand francs and the admiring friendship of Lloyds' cashier."

"You got three thousand francs, have you?" Captain Rocca, the human avalanche, stopped and began to giggle quietly to himself.

"What's the big idea? Come on along to Gruber's." The Loot frowned at his companion's evident inability to terminate his fit of giggling.

The parade halted in front of Gruber's restaurant. "Listen, Avalanche, before we go another step farther—and I don't mean an orphan's parents——"

"I know. Soft A as in salmon."

"What did you bring that fish subject up for?"

"Go ahead and say what you were going to say."

"I wasn't going to say anything. I was going to ask something."

"Well, ask it. I'm lissen."

Fifteen Hundred Bucks 193

"All I wanted to ask was, do all your folks have these laughing fits?"

"You know what I was laughing at? Forgive me, Loot, for laughing. I couldn't help it. Three thousand francs is a lot of money—but how much is twenty million dollars in francs? You're an Engineer. You ought to be able to figure that out."

"Hundred million francs."

"More'n that. Loot, I guess it was rotten bad manners to giggle, but we got a hundred million francs of my money to buy lunch with if we need it. I'm a lousy millionaire. Made it in California. If we run short after we spend my twenty million, there's an army bank roll behind us. All I'm doing on this trip is buyin' lunch for the army. One-man raid on local food supplies. Olive oil, raisins, hay for horses——"

"T for thirsty,—come on in here. Between your mere millions and my own three thousand francs we can pay for the drinks some way. Look out for that step, Avalanche."

Inside the Gruber establishment, after the adroit and sympathetic veteran of Verdun had served the first frigid and dynamic cocktails, the Loot suggested food.

"Hold the deal, old ravenous," his companion protested. "My motto is, Never eat on an empty stomach. A few trifling rations after another twenty or forty of these little wonders—yes. But at the moment, no." The Avalanche sighed a sigh of deep content. "Loot, I mentioned troubles. Forget it. I haven't got any more troubles than a jackrabbit—that is to say, I wish five or six of 'em were right here with us now. By the way, who were your troubles? You said you had some. Who were they?"

The Loot tried to remember his troubles. Failing in this, "I must have mislaid them, Avalanche . . . I'm glad I met you. After lunch we prowl around and to-night I want you to join on in what may be an outstanding event in the history of Bordeaux."

"I'm signed for the cruise. Where's old Alexander?"

Alexander at the moment was helping a reception committee of his fellow employees. The group, in mass formation, bowed low in

Fifteen Hundred Bucks 195

welcome to a swarthy gentleman who looked like a bullfighter in plain clothes. At the bullfighter's side, enjoying her protector's protection, walked a Perfectly Beautiful Girl.

The parade headed in the general direction of the Loot and his companion. It halted three paces from the Loot's table while, with gestures, the veteran of Verdun explained to the frowning bullfighter the sorrow which destroyed him by reason of the deplorable, the impossible, calamity.

"What calamity does Alexander mean?" Captain Rocca inquired.

"Vinegar-face telephoned a luncheon reservation for this table and got the wrong number. He is timed with a short fuse and will explode in about four seconds."

"Let him explode and to hell with him," the quartermaster captain returned with a smile.

"Steady, you Avalanche—there's a lady with him."

Captain Rocca craned his neck around the silken upholstery of the partition at the end of the wall seat of his sanctuary, and then, echoing an inspiration to which the Loot had already reacted, "Holy old goldfish, orate some diplomatic language and get 'em over here!"

Before the impetuous Avalanche had finished speaking the Loot was on his feet. There followed some Chesterfieldian hypocrisy with gestures. Midway of the scene the Loot was glad that he had taken time out of the overstressed morning to shave, and that his tailor was a good tailor.

It developed that a foursome was a most admirable arrangement, but none of the quartet was as well pleased from the outward evidence as the clucking veteran of Verdun.

Forthwith, under the affectionate supervision of Alexander, school let out and the merry laughter of little children gratified teacher's heart.

"That's all right about your real name, darling," Captain Rocca protested to the feminine member of the quartet. "You are saccharine and peachlike. As far as I'm concerned your name is Little Saccharine. The loveliest thing about you is that your saccharine qualities do much to offset the general effect of your vinegar-faced companion."

"I the English speak, and do not understand you," the bullfighter cut in at this point.

"Don't listen. Talk to the Loot. Me and your girl are getting along fine without you," Avalanche rejoined.

Within the hour the party craved more hell room. "There is a beautiful wildwood retreat furnished with quaint ice and spreading chestnut trees out on the edge of town," Avalanche suggested. "Leave us pass a given point and parade in that direction, where roistering in the great outdoors may be roistered by one and all without help from the M. P. gang."

"On your way, Avalanche, and don't think up any more language to delay the game. Let's go!"

At the Bower of Eden, on the edge of Bordeaux, a grove of old trees offered a refreshing oasis of shade wherein thirsty travelers might rest; and here, away from the fevered activities of the city, the quartet went into camp. There were wide tables and comfortable chairs under the old trees, and other tables on platforms supported by gnarled branches. Steep stairways, little better than ladders, led to these elevated sanctuaries where, twenty feet above the ground, adventurous spirits might make merry.

"It is called the Bower of Eden," a grizzled waiter explained to the inquisitive Avalanche. "Madame Eve suffered her fall from that highest platform which you see above you."

"We will rally round the table from which Eve fell. Serve the next dozen bottles to us up there."

"Bien, M'sieur. But Madame——"

"Madame has been a dancer," the bullfighter interposed, "can walk a tight rope and will be quite at home on her elevated perch. Is it not so, my little cabbage?"

The little cabbage answered with action instead of words. She ran up the stairway. She kicked her slippers right and left into the great beyond. She vaulted over the railing of the high platform, landing lightly on a twelve-inch branch which extended into the leafy jungles of lighter foliage. On this doubtful footing she poised with perfect confidence. "I am a little chimpanzee!" she announced. "Cha-cha-cha grrr-eeet! Where are the mighty hunters of Africa? With champagne corks make the shooting!"

Target practice consumed three bottles, and then the firing at the actual objective began. Waiters lugged another dozen bottles of champagne to the mighty hunters. The bombardment lasted for half an hour and was terminated by the little chimpanzee's declaration of surrender. "But not once was I hit. I capitulate with honor because of a growing thirst." In along the sloping branch of the tree danced Little Saccharine, to a salvo of popping corks which promised to terminate her thirst.

Silly business, all of it, the Loot reflected, coming sanely to the surface for an instant. "Leave us ramble gayly in the rubber-tired hack to the Chapeau Rouge," he invited. "Little ol' dinner of herbs with a mess of pottage."

Avalanche hiccuped heartily and voted yes. "Hooray for li'l ol' mess of pottage. C'mon here, you Li'l Saccharine. We will never leave each other. I can drive ol' hack."

Climbing into the car, "I'll drive ol' hack," Avalanche insisted. "Never knew what it was to be a father, but I've got eight little cars of my own. Maybe ten or fifteen. Git in the back seat, Loot, with that bullfighter. Me an' Li'l Saccharine Chimpanzee gonna ride up here. Hang on tight and see what a speed demon can do——"

The speed demon's first move was to back the car heavily into a stone wall which had stood the stresses of three centuries. "My mistake. Pardon me," the Avalanche apologized. "Sense of direction is all it takes. Hang on tight—we're gonna start the other way."

The start ahead was made under a full throttle that threatened to disintegrate the rubber-tired hack until, coming back sweetly, the clutch translated a shivering earthquake into lateral motion.

"What nationality are you?" the Loot asked the companion to his left.

"Portuguese—but not afraid to die."

"Neither am I—say, you didn't mean to insinuate I was afraid to die or anything, did you?"

"I am unaccustomed to such vehemence. The gentleman would do well to control his tones in speaking to one in whose veins flows——"

Bang! Merely a lamp-post.

After the fender had been straightened and when the car was again lined out in its run toward the Chapeau Rouge, the argument in the back seat was resumed. It developed with simplicity and directness to a crisis which found the Loot sitting securely on the huddled remains of the gentleman in whose veins flowed the best blood of his country.

A yelp from the Loot sounded high above the clattering noises of the speeding car. "Yeow! Oooo—yowch!"

"'S'matter?" This from Avalanche, who was driving with one hand.

Saccharine Chimpanzee peered coyly over the Avalanche's shoulder. "Mon Dieu! Regard, if you please, the scene behind you."

In the bottom of the car the huddled representative of all that was best in blue blood was gnashing his teeth and spitting forth shreds of O. D. uniform.

Perched high in the back seat, the Loot was holding on with one hand and rubbing the back of his lap with the other. "Ooo-ouch. He bit me in the tonneau!"

Avalanche stopped the car. "Whaddya mean he bit you?"

"He bit right through these pants," the Loot complained. "Feels like blood poison has set in."

Avalanche reached around and took hold of Portugal with both hands. He lifted the snarling and incoherent member of the quartet clean over the side of the car and released him to a running start. "How does it feel now, Loot?" Avalanche inquired with deep sympathy in his voice.

"It feels lots better. Hurry up or we'll be late for supper."

When the car skidded to a stop eighty feet past the entrance to the Chapeau Rouge, Little Saccharine called the roll. "Where is my protector?" she inquired without much real interest.

"Old Vinegar-face is irreproachably lost," Avalanche informed her. "Lissen, baby— you got a couple of the best protectors in the world. Don't you remember what happened back there where Vinegar-face bit the Loot and blood poison set in? Couldn't of been more than two minutes ago."

"It is nothing. He will be along presently. He always catches up. I lost him in Africa once, before we were married, and for two thousand miles——"

"Married! You don't mean you and that bullfighter are married? I never heard of such a thing. The idea! A fine little girl like you——"

"Of a certainty. He is the Prince de Cherida, and I am his princess. His name is Jack."

"Well, good heavens!" Avalanche scratched his head in deep thought. He looked up at the Princess and the Loot. "Well, heavens on earth! That makes it all different. Let's not stand here on the sidewalk . . . I tell you what—let's eat."

"Yeah—let's eat. We don't want to keep a princess waiting. C'mon, Princess."

"I kinda thought you was a princess," the Avalanche offered, and then, in a hoarse whisper to the Loot, "Pssst! Loot, what do you suppose princesses eat?"

"Miscellaneous groceries, you hippopotamus. Git in the door there."

Recognizing the Loot, after appropriate felicitations had been exchanged, "Covers for your party of twenty are laid in the Louis Quatorze suite upstairs," the rotund management announced.

Recovering quickly, "They will be along presently," the Loot returned.

When the festive throng arrived at the Louis Quatorze suite it consisted of the Loot and the Princess. Avalanche had sidetracked himself and doubled back in a hurried search for an appropriate and congenial personnel to fill the vacant chairs.

Inspired by old man Trouble, "An anchovy, perhaps, with our next cocktail?" the Loot suggested, "or an infant sardine on toast? Do you like sardines?"

This polite inquiry, it appeared, was a brazen insult. Little Saccharine, reverting to chimpanzee language, chattered on for a while and then hissed herself into a fit of sobbing, through all of which the Loot stared at her with widening eyes. "What the hell? Listen now, Princess——"

But the Saccharine Princess had no opportunity to listen, for the wide doors of the Louis Quatorze suite had opened and through them poured a parade of naval officers. Following the procession, lurching a little at times to starboard and port, swept the majestic Avalanche. "Here's our guests, Loot," he called loudly. "Lemme introduce the Navy. All of 'em old friends of mine—dear old college chums."

"When do we eat?" the Navy inquired.

"Never eat on an empty stomach." The Avalanche reiterated his slogan to an appreciative audience. "My motto is——"

The motto was smothered under an armload of Princess, who sought a manly chest and sympathy. While the Loot milled around with his new consignment of guests the Princess told her story to the Avalanche. "Yes indeed, Little Saccharine," the Avalanche agreed, "nothing but a brazen insult. I agree with you entirely. Come over here and I'll make the Loot apologize."

He led the Princess over toward the Lieutenant. "Listen, Loot," Little Saccharine's champion began, "you insulted this little girl. You asked her if she liked sardines and you know doggone well her impoverished husband sells sardines, no matter if he is the prince of whatever town it is. You ought to be ashamed of yourself for bringing up a sardine subject to a princess when her impoverished husband sells sardines. Look at her. Almost on the verge of tears."

The Loot smiled deliberately at the Princess, and something in his smile won the day for him. "Get off that verge of tears, darling. Have a drink. I don't even remember of having have had——"

"Loot, what you tryin' to say?"

The Loot blinked quickly and continued in better control of his vocal organs. "—remember of having had the pleasure of meeting your husband."

"You forgetful little rascal!" The Princess smiled coyly. "Do you not remember that he bit you in the tonneau?"

"Call it tonneau if you will,——"

"Ceash you babbling," the Avalanche admonished the Princess and the Loot. "Admiral got to speak a toast."

Anticipating the probability of having to let go all his shore lines for the balance of the night, one of the navy gentlemen became verbally sentimental to a degree which inspired tears here and there in his audience. "And it is with tenderness and longing, our memory turning ever to those hallowed scenes—" He extended his lifted glass toward the entrance to the Louis Quatorze suite. As he did this the doors opened and in galloped the remains of Prince Vinegarface, not so noble at the moment, but still competent to inquire with dramatic intensity for his old feudal opponent, the Loot.

"In the name of my outraged heritage of pride, I demand him to stand forth!"

The Prince raised himself on tiptoe and surveyed the crowd, but failed to discover his victim. Then, slightly annoyed, the Avalanche emerged from the company and grasped the arm of the prince. "Come in this room with me a minute, Jack," he suggested, lending a three-hundred-pound muscular impulse to his verbal suggestion. "We got to hold a powley-wowley." Over his shoulder, as he disappeared with his protesting captive, "Powley-wowley is sardine talk for pow-wow," the Avalanche explained.

"What makes the little desperado so vicious?" one of the navy men inquired.

"He'll be all right after he talks to that big dove of peace," the Lieutenant returned. "He's a prince that got insulted and bit me on the leg. Have a drink. On with the dance. . . . Gentlemen, I have the honor to propose the health of the fairest and dearest lady in our midst, Little Saccharine, Princess de Cherida!"

At the climax of a vociferous tribute, true to the Loot's prediction, from their retreat, arm in arm and both singing "He's My Pal," came the Prince and the Avalanche.

Heading straight for the Loot, the Prince began an elaborate apology for his part in the biting business.

"Forget it, old-timer . . . here's luck!"

The peace conference was rudely interrupted by a sudden chorus from the Navy: "When do we eat!" whereupon the Avalanche took it upon himself to order the dinner served. The repast proved to be a sketchy affair, but it floated high on copious billows of gratifying refreshments and, as the Navy afterwards explained, the company "managed to swim through it."

The dinner and its array of liquids was followed by a rapid retreat to the Double-track Tunnel, which lay some blocks away from the Chapeau Rouge. Within an hour the impromptu vaudeville purveyed by this slightly shopworn subterranean establishment had palled and the march was resumed toward the Apollo Theater.

Here, after a brief and conspicuous appearance, the party was led backstage by the Loot.

While the Navy and the Apollo chorus accomplished a quick affiliation, the Avalanche gratified his longing for histrionic fame by staging an impromptu bullfight with an agitated stage manager who finally surrendered to overwhelming odds and went through with a noteworthy imitation of a bull while the Avalanche performed in his best toreador manner.

For the audience that night the show included half a dozen novel and refreshing turns whose advertising value bulged the box office for weeks thereafter. It was observed that the chorus dwindled with each appearance until, of the original forty dancers, hardly more than half were on the stage.

The Toreador, in one of his gyrations, encountered the Loot. "Looks like a big night."

"Listen, you savage, the Navy is anchored fast enough, and they won't leave here till the house goes dark. Round up Vinegar-face and the Princess and let's beat it."

"That's a good idea. He wants us to go down to his boat, anyhow."

"Has he got a boat?"

"Best little yacht in the harbor. Find Little Saccharine and I'll get Vinegar-face and us quartet makes a side-door exit."

"Fair enough. Make it snappy."

The Prince's yacht turned out to be a hundred-ton schooner smelling strongly of sardines. A lull in the shipboard festivities gave place to a polite family altercation between the Prince and Little Saccharine, at the conclusion of which, with what seemed to the Loot to be a somewhat gratuitous eloquence, the flame of jealousy ignited a vocabulary of hypocrisy in the Prince's narrow chest. "Take this lady," he concluded, addressing himself to the Loot. "She is yours! And, as you say, to hell with her!"

The Prince grasped Little Saccharine's hand where it clutched his arm and extended the trophy of victory toward the winner.

"How do you get that way!" The Loot recalled the painful incident of having been bitten in the tonneau. He turned to the Avalanche, who, sleepy-eyed, was observing the scene with painful lack of interest. "This guy and his likker haven't amalgamated. Dangerous hombre. Avalanche, you and me leave right now."

The Avalanche blinked his approval of the suggestion. "Let's go."

On shore, in the cold gray dawn, when the Avalanche had been delivered to his hotel, the Loot spoke his farewells. "Grand little party, you old Avalanche."

"Loot, you and me both! Lissen—I arranged with Vinegar-face to send your outfit some sardines with my compliments," the Avalanche announced. "Parting gift I give you in memory of the best little old party I've had since I joined the war. Had a grand time. So long, old-timer!"

The Loot started away in his rubber-tired hack. Alone, he headed for his camp. By the time he arrived, the events of the night had taken on some of the qualities of a dream. Feeling not so good, he undressed and rolled into bed for an early morning nap. "Wake me up at nine o'clock," he said to one of the orderlies on duty, and then he drifted into a broken sleep which was interrupted by fleeting recurrent memories of the night which had passed.

Late in the afternoon to the Gang's quarters came nauseating rumors concerning a fishy addition to the army ration. Facing Jugger and Rags and Patsy, Isadog issued a bulletin. "Jimmy the Ink just told me the Loot is signing personal receipts for them sardines. Eight truckloads of 'em! All the sardines in the world—and lissen to one of Uncle Salmon's heroes: This fish war has got me fed up. Fish ain't no treat to me, and the Loot is sidetracked in the bean if he thinks sardines will soften the curse."

"Sneak around the cookhouse and see what's goin' on. Ask Shorty what he's got to say."

"Shorty's busy cookin'—you know how he is if you poke your nose into his joint this time of day. Well, part of the army is mighty apt to pull a walkout if they's fish for supper."

"Git calm."

Within an hour, none too robust as a result of the Bordeaux passes, the Gang experienced a recurrence of the sentiments which had characterized their first hour on shipboard. Retreat found them sulky and silent.

Immediately after Retreat, not caring to inflict any supper upon himself, the Loot retired to his office, where, making up for lost time and wrestling with an oversized fit of katzenjammers, Jimmy the Ink sat at his desk in front of an insurmountable stack of paper work. Across the room, peering gloomily out of a window, stood Spike Randall.

The Loot greeted these two military marvels, and then to the Top, "What's the matter, Spike? How come the rain cloud all over your map?"

"Loot, I'm worried about the Gang. They're ready to blow up on the sardine question."

At that moment from the Gang's mess shack there broke a sudden rumble of voices. The frown on Spike Randall's face deepened, and it was followed by an apprehensive look. "Lissen!—it sounds like the dam has bust!"

The Gang roared out another cheer, at which Spike started for the door. "You stay here, Loot," he said. "I'll pacify those babies or come back feet first."

The Loot smiled. "Stand steady, you grief-eater! That yell isn't a battle cry. Sidetrack your sardine conscience. I traded the whole damned sardine tonnage to our blackface labor battalions for enough T-bone steaks to last the Gang from now on. The way she lays, for the next six months we draw the biggest beef ration in the A. E. F. Git calm and dry those tears. There'll be no strike to-night."

Chapter 7

THAT AIN'T NO LADY

AFTER the big false alarm epidemic had quieted, and when the front and Siberia and the good old U. S. A. stuff had dissolved in the early fall rains of France, the Gang settled down to a season of plain hard work.

With their storage depot half completed, contemplating another year or so of prosaic construction, the old-timers renewed affiliations throughout the local countryside and prepared for a hard winter. Numerous promotions which involved separation from the outfit were scorned or side-stepped by potential victims and officer material developed enough spontaneous stupidity to justify the cancellation of whatever glowing recommendations the Loot had forwarded through military channels.

Except for Corporal Badger, all of the A. W. O. Lephants—big-leave men—came drifting back and the Battle of Bordeaux was resumed with renewed enthusiasm where it had been interrupted by the distant enemy.

Then, all set to break their previous records of various sorts, overnight and without warning the Gang were uprooted and planted in a new field of activity where another flock of warehouses and tracks were required.

Among a hundred other minor details, "Round up Corporal Badger," the Loot directed, and forthwith the call for the absentee was relayed through mysterious channels with sufficient velocity and weight to lend the culprit a momentum which brought him back to the fold from the sunlit sanctuary which he had enjoyed on the north coast of Africa.

"What's the big idea?" Corporal Badger inquired, blinking his petulance boldly in Spike Randall's face.

"The big idea is we're goin' to shoot you just as soon as we get some of this local grief off our hands," the Top returned, busy with his duties in the Gang's new environment.

"You stick around. There's going to be a muster and you damn near had us balled up the last time. If the Loot hadn't answered when your name was called, about six of us would have gone to jail."

"What about all the back pay I've got comin' for the last five months?"

"One more crack like that and I'll soak you in the jaw. Jimmy the Ink has forged your name for you bokoo times, including one little document that turns your lousy coin over to the company fund. We got to make a profit on you some way."

Corporal Badger blinked at the Top in silence for ten seconds, and then began to cry softly to himself.

"Out of here!" the Top roared. "I know you for the stew-bum weeper you are. Get to hell out of this office. And listen, you sugar-face wino—don't pull no sob story on this outfit. We're wise to you, and the complaint department is fed up. You been nothin' but a lousy liability since you signed on, and you've dodged your work and for a plugged clacker I'd knock the block off of one Badger casualty and mingle his fragments into the scenery so that your next-of-kin couldn't recognize nothin' but your purple beak. Get to hell out of here, but stick around like I told you."

Corporal Badger blinked the tears out of his eyes and saluted the Top in a military manner. "You remind me so much of an officer when you talk that way." The tearful one reached in his hip pocket and hauled out a compact bale of French currency. "Sir, Corporal Badger requests the Sergeant to take care of this roll for him so that Corporal Badger can avoid temptation when the game begins to-night."

"For the love of the holy blond greenbacks! —how much you got there?"

The tearful Badger saluted again. "Sir, there are forty big pictures and a lot of small ones—mebbe a total of fifty thousand francs. I remember I had close to a hundred thousand after I bust the Navy at Marseilles. . . . but Africa is so expensive. Then there was the boat I chartered to bring me across, and the airplane from the blue Mediterranean into

That Ain't No Lady 221

this drizzly climate—if there's fifty thousand francs there, it will be a surprise——"

"Shut up!" Spike Randall was auditing the bank roll. "Don't bother me . . . go on outside and stick around like I told you. Go report to the Loot. Go any place, only get out of here!"

After the first count had been verified, the Top breathed one deep sigh. "Better than seventy thousand francs——"

He stared into vacancy for a moment, but his meditation was interrupted by the return of Corporal Badger, who again saluted with the right hand, while with his left he extended a thin blue slip of paper toward his keeper.

"Sir, I forgot about this," he said. "My folks sent me some more money for expenses. I would be much obliged if you would keep it safe for me."

Spike Randall inspected the blue slip of paper and discovered that it was a draft for a mere five thousand dollars. "Very well, Badger," he said gruffly. "Very well, Mister Rockefeller Morgan Badger. Get out of this office like I told you. Frisk yourself, and if you find any more trifles,—frisk yourself now so you won't have to come back."

Corporal Badger saluted again. "Sir, I'm sorry to report that that is all I have."

"Then get out."

Saluting again, the tearful one stepped out and experienced some relief when a work detail gobbled him up and relieved him of any further immediate responsibility relative to his checkered career.

Laden with the truant's treasure, Spike Randall sought the Lieutenant in the latter's new office at the far end of the Headquarters hut. "Loot," he announced, "the wandering Badger just hove in, all festooned with remorse and cash."

The Top handed over the trophy of his encounter with Corporal Badger. "Over seventy thousand francs, and this check for five thousand dollars."

The Loot smiled grimly. "Our wandering boy is paying a dividend. I'll keep it for him till after the company barks a reply to the roll call at Retreat."

"Mebbe you better bank it permanent for him. He can spoil a lot of organization if your turn him loose with that roll."

"We can't do anything—he's busted his best records starting from zero more than once, and this heavyweight cash from his people shows up every time we get the halter on him."

"Right!" the Top agreed. "That's that. I've got a lot more bad news, Loot."

"Spring it. Grief is my dish."

"You remember that bunch of scab replacements they sent us before we moved up here?—Well, there's another mess of 'em out there, just as bad or worse. There's twenty in this detail—and of all the jailbirds and yeggs and dips I ever saw, this outfit cops the ball and chain! They've been here only two hours, but the commissary till has been cracked already and five watches are missing up to date. What are we goin' to do about it?"

The Loot smiled, and something in his smile suggested the triumph of mind over military matters. He reached for a letter on his desk and handed it to Spike Randall. "The devil takes care of his own. Read that letter. The Department of Criminal Investigation needs more detectives to cope with the crime wave that's hit the A. E. F. Read what they want: 'keen, intelligent men who can be trusted.' What about it?"

"We win again. This outfit is the keenest bunch of crooks I've ever seen, intelligent enough to lift Isadog's wrist watch off him in the middle of a gesture, and as far as trusting them goes—you can absolutely trust each and every one of 'em all the way from burglary to the electric chair. I'll have a truck ready in ten minutes."

"And we'll boon the D. C. I. with a couple of tons of assorted detective talent. That's that—and to-morrow we forget these military matters and start to work. They're sending us a thousand enemy prisoners, one labor battalion and a smear of Annamites. Have a look at the new plans when you get a chance— fifty warehouses, tracks to serve them, and camp enough to furnish room and board for the hired men. We'll run the same organization here as we did in the Gironde country."

A week later, strung out for a mile along one section of the Gang's new construction project, a thousand fat and sassy enemy prisoners toyed with a piece of new track.

The heavy juggling incident to grading, distribution of ties and rail, and spiking the line had been accomplished by singing crews of track-layers from a blackface labor battalion. Now, free from the menace of cruel and unusual punishment in the form of hard work, the enemy contingent tamped a little ballast under the low ties here and there, heaved out kinks and listlessly bolted up the angle bars.

The thousand enemy prisoners worked under the supervision of Old Pop Sibley, Patsy and Mike. Superfluous moral support for this trio was afforded by a platoon of British guards whose military bearing offered a startling contrast to the rough-and-ready sartorial equipment of salvaged clothing worn by the trio in charge of the work.

The November morning was clear and frosty. The British guards were gathered around a dozen warming fires. For a while, beginning their morning's work, the prisoners hit the ball with sufficient ardor to get warmed up, and then all along the line the pace slacked until Pop Sibley galvanized the outfit with a heartfelt oration wherein his charges were promised a homemade consignment of the horrors of war.

"Soon der war iss finished," an affable German corporal explained to Pop Sibley. "Unt den mit der track no more ve vork."

"Hit the ball, you bristle-necked beer keg! You ain't in no war. You're in my army now! Lean on that tampin' bar before I bend it around your belly."

Der liebe Gott im Himmel! Could these American savages never understand any of the finer things of life?

At eleven o'clock, faintly from Rochelle and from the harbor at La Pallice came a sustained alarm. Sirens and whistles shrieked their message loudly enough for all the countryside to hear.

The Armistice was a fact. The war was done.

At first, outwardly cold, the Gang gave no exhibition of the emotions which the eleven-o'clock alarm had awakened, but later in the day when the unreal element of the great event had in some measure disappeared, enthusiastic planning for their immediate future engaged the outfit's attention.

"Couple of weeks more and good morning, San Francisco!"

"It'll take longer than that—a week to get ready and a week to go across the lousy ocean, and mebbe another week after that. I figger us birds won't hit the Pacific Coast much inside of three weeks from now."

"How long is a piece of rope—that's how long it'll take you to git back."

The last man's estimate found verification in an order issued the next day whereby the Gang was transferred to a new and desolate location in the dismal swamps back of Bordeaux.

"Anyhow, this is a good place to rest."

But there were more buildings to be built, and many miles of highway to be patched and the second winter closed in with a work program which promised to add another pair of service stripes to the three which then adorned the arms of the outfit.

"Never mind," the philosophers commented. "The harder they work us the more we play."

Then, under a new régime inaugurated by hard-boiled authority, there was no play. Discipline tightened in the Base, and Bordeaux passes were no longer tickets to happiness. "They's a new guy runnin' the police force, and what d'you suppose he did? The first thing he wrote was a order where you git pinched if you're seen with a femme. Walkin' on the street or any place else with a gal, and some M. P. gits you. Don't make no difference if it's a lady from the 'Y' or a Red Cross entertainer or nothin'."

"That's only half of it. There's another order out that says only perfect little gentlemen git to go home. You got to be an angel or you're gonna miss the boat. Jimmy the Ink says the best-behaved birds go home first."

"That don't bother us none—we got another five or ten years' work on these roads in sunny France, like a bunch of convicts."

"You hear what that M. P. outfit did to us birds yesterday? Me and Riff and Rags was having a glass of beer in Gruber's, and in come one of Major MacFlinty's pets, and before we got done with him that beer cost all three of us two-thirds off for three months."

"Who the hell is Major MacFlinty?"

"He's the new king snipe that's runnin' the police force around the Base."

"I'll tell the cockeyed world he runs his lousy police force! No more Bordeaux for me," another victim announced. "Right this minute the Loot has charge sheets of a court-martial on his desk that has me workin' for my rations for the next year. And all I done was try to take Madeleine out for a ride in a hack. I never knew nothing about that order about femmes until it bust right in my face, and when it did it blew my name clear off the pay roll from now on."

"Well, they give you a vaudeville show every night right here in camp to keep you pacified, and you got to say they ain't no kick about tobacco and candy any more——"

"Yeah—well, we ain't never had to kick about candy since old man Smith sent the company that carload, and we manage to thrive up a little tobacco now and then. As far as vaudeville goes, there's plenty of talent right in the Gang. They ain't no funnier show in the world than Isadog and his talkin' dummy act. They can take their damn imported vaudeville and their welfare stuff and their uplift and to hell with it as far as I'm concerned. When we needed it most they didn't come across, and don't you forget it."

"Anybody ever write a letter to old man Smith thanking him for that carload of candy he sent us when we needed welfare so bad?"

"We was too busy. That was away back in the early days."

"Somebody ought to write him a letter."

"You sound like a Uplifter. A letter would be a fat bunch of thanks for a carload of candy. The least we can do is send him a good souvenir."

"Let's pass the hat and send that white man a high-toned marble clock for the parlor or something."

"He's got clocks all over his house. Chances is he'd like a good marble statue to stick around some place. These Frogs are noted for sculping."

"Sure he would. I saw some swell statues of nude dames down in the museum. Better sculping than you ever saw on any tombstone in your life."

"Where d'you git the tombstone stuff? Send him a good cheerful statue."

"You birds are all sidetracked. If you want to send him something that ties in with France there's only one thing to send him, and that's Joan of Arc. She's the most historical character the country ever saw. She's just like George Washington. Lots of class. It's a cinch old man Smith would relish a good Joan of Arc. We could make Cawpril Badger put up the price. He's lousy with jack."

"Does the Loot know about her? I mean, is she a notorious enough character to have the Loot O. K. passes for a couple of squads to go out looking for this statue?"

"Of course he knows about her—everybody knows about her. She got on a horse one night and saved the entire nation of France."

"Well, listen—I don't crave to pollute any pure and holy sentimental ideas with what you might call practical things, but it seems to me if this Joan of Ark is the heavyweight you claim she is, we ought to be able to graft bokoo passes off the Loot to hunt for this statue of that gal."

"Hooray for a big idea! This spikes them M. P. birds. That boy has brains."

"Git a committee."

"Nix on the mob scene. Where's Pop Sibley? Let old Pop Sibley spring this on the Loot and he's bound to win."

The plot was amplified forthwith, and after half an hour's coaching Pop Sibley felt himself qualified to recite a plausible tale which would stand up under the Loot's questioning, whereby passes for thirty or forty men could be obtained on the strength of a search for a suitable statue of the heroine.

A twenty-mile radius, four points of the compass, seven or eight villages in and about each point, Joan on horseback and afoot, in marble, concrete, bronze, wood, iron or plaster—there were enough variables to warrant a search which would require the time of at least forty of the Old Guard.

"And lissen, Pop, if the Loot craves to know how come we got to spread out so much and asks you why not get a statue from some sculptor that sculps them, tell him that old man Smith is a fanatic on antique statues and don't want anything new. If he gets to wondering about the company fund and asks you where the money is coming from to buy it with, tell him we passed the hat and got a thousand dollars."

Reminded of a detail which he had overlooked, the speaker summoned Corporal Badger. "Listen, louse," he said, "you got a thousand dollars for this Joan of Arc project, haven't you?"

Corporal Badger nodded affably. "Sure— I still got that blue check that I can get cashed as soon as I get unconfined from camp. I got to serve another week yet."

"You give Pop Sibley that check right now, and next week when your time is up you go down to Bordeaux with him and give him that thousand dollars. You better give him some more for us birds' expenses. We'll need bokoo jack chasing around on this deal. You better give Pop another five hundred for expense money, and we'll put your name down on the list when we send it to old man Smith with the statue."

"That's all right," Corporal Badger agreed. "I'll donate that much, but just as soon as I get that check cashed I'm going to need a lot of expense money myself. I don't want to be mean about it, but I announce right now that I'm mighty short of cash."

"Yeah, he's down to his last million." A harsh critic voiced the Gang's opinion of the truant Badger.

Immediately after his interview with the Loot, old Pop Sibley returned to the waiting Gang and made his report. "Loot said yes. He thought it was a first-class scheme and a mighty nice thing to do to send Mr. Smith a old antique of Joan of Arc. He said anything he could do to count on him for. Only thing he said was not to spread out too much at one time. He thought the committee better sort of flock around in one town for a while, and then move on like seven-year locusts to some place else, and not everybody go in different directions all at once. He telephoned down to the Base while I was standin' there and got the brass neck's O. K. on the deal, and all your passes will git the blue stamp."

Old Pop Sibley paused and looked about him. He took a deep breath, and then: "By gum, boys, as fur as we're concerned it looks like this cruel war is over! It is moved and seconded that the general sense of this here meeting is three cheers for Joan of Arc and to hell with the M. P. police force."

The epidemic of Joan of Arc passes began in a comparatively mild way, but within a week it was raging in a manner which did much to offset the strictures imposed by the new régime of Major MacFlinty and his prowling aides.

Pairs, trios, quartets and mob details, ostensibly in search of art for art's sake, rambled safely through the Base, displaying their passes upon demand and gloating heartily after each triumph over Major MacFlinty's pests. Then, comparing notes, a gang of M. P.'s discovered the obvious fact that most of the cares which infested their professional days emanated from one source. A protest, forwarded through military channels, reached the Loot.

"Round up these Joan of Arc tourists when you get a chance and tell 'em to concentrate on one district at a time," he instructed the Top. "Our little playmates on the police force are getting fed up. They're kicking about simultaneous riots at Libourne, and San Loubes and Cubesac, and you can't blame them for it. Another thing, Spike—it seems to me that the big Joan of Arc campaign ought to begin to show some tangible results."

The Loot's message reached the Gang at a most inopportune time. Most of the Badger money was gone and so was he, but six heavy winners who had come out of an infantry regiment's pay day with cash enough to justify six separate and distinct celebrations, protested that the Loot's untimely advice cramped their style.

At this, rallying nobly, old Pop Sibley came to the surface out of the slough of despond with a gilt-edged scheme calculated to afford the six eager capitalists opportunity to function with true Southern hospitality.

"I got a cheap old antique wooden Joan of Arc on a horse located at Izon," he announced. "The horse comes apart. First there's a hind leg and another hind leg, and his belly and his front legs and his neck. Then his head unscrews off his neck, then Joan of Arc is sort of standing up in the stirrups and waving a sword. The sword comes out of her hand, and that arm she is waving the sword with unscrews off her chest. How many trips does that make altogether? . . . Never mind; I know it will take half a dozen trips to get the horse, let alone getting this here wooden lady. You men kin git action. She and the horse is both as big as life size, and there's no reason why you birds can't give a party at that little restaurant in Izon every time we get a leg or a stummick off that horse to bring back here in the Loot's Dodge. We can have just as good a time at Izon as any place in the world. The grub and the likker is first-class, and that back dining room is big enough to hold everybody that you gents can afford to invite. How about it?"

It was obvious that the scheme had its merits, and the Gang realized that the winter of their discontent was to be enlightened by six more promising events wherein joy for the moment would be more or less unconfined.

"Let Pop Sibley ask the Loot for the passes," some one suggested. "He can tell the truth and get the Loot calmed down by saying at last we have found the Joan of Arc we want."

Pop Sibley considered the matter. "About how many passes do you figger you need on this horse and Joan of Arc detail?"

After a brief survey of the possibilities, a

conservative element cut the wholesalers down to a reasonable request. "Ask him to O. K. three squads. Tell him it's a mighty big horse. Tell him how big horses was in France in those days."

"Don't tell him nothing about it being wood. Ask him what he figgers a cast-iron horse weighs, so he can sidetrack his brain on the specific gravity of horse meat and pile-driver hammers. The minute he reaches for his slide rule, tell him there's three squads in the Joan of Arc committee."

"The Loot won't reach for no slide rule—he'll squinch his eyes up and figger within a pound of what the horse weighs in his bean. You got to make it snappy while he's thinkin'."

The first raid was a success, but after the fifth request for passes for the Joan of Arc detail, "What's the big idea?" the Loot inquired. "How many encores are you playing on the Joan of Arc bet?"

"Lieutenant, the first trip we got a hind leg and the second trip we got another hind leg of the horse——"

"I've heard all of that. What the hell kind of a centipede is that horse? You've brought five hind legs in so far. Round up the rest of that animal and make it snappy. The provost marshal is on my trail right now, and if we crave any standing in this military community we've got to tighten up."

Subsequently, in council, "What's eatin' on the Loot, do you suppose? You think Major MacFlinty has got his goat?"

"Nobody ain't got his goat, but lissen, Gang—Jimmy the Ink told me that yesterday when the Loot was riding that little welfare queen to the Chapeau Rouge for lunch in his rubber-tired hack, he got messed up with three of the MacFlinty rattlesnakes and had to yell loud enough for the Base Commander to hear him before he got loose."

"You mean them birds pinched the Loot?"

"Not only pinched him, but held him till the old General told 'em to lay off. Chuck said the layout had the Loot flabbergasted. First time it ever happened."

In the ensuing silence old Pop Sibley clucked a couple of times. "Boys, that there outrage is news to me," he announced; and then: "The time has come to strike a blow fer freedom! I got an idea and it's a whale. My motto is, Give me liberty or send me home!" Outburst of cheering. "Git calm;—Rabble, I need Isadog and another desperate volunteer to help guide us children of sorrow out of the wilderness. Who'll come along, survive or perish, to help me eradicate these here M. P.'s that have us free men hogtied with the chains of slavery?"

A hundred voices answered in unison.

"You sound like you used to before you got military. Isadog, you win without no contest. Front and center. Chuck, I got to use you and the Loot's Dodge,—stand out here. Jugger, you never yet laid down against no odds. You're elected! Gents, Jugger and Isadog, Chuck and me hereby swears to do or die. If our foot slips, lay a little wreath of roses on the jail. If we got any luck you can bet your last clacker the MacFlinty police force will be a bitter memory when we finish, instead of the heartbreakin' scourge that now makes life a burden."

"What's the layout, Pop?"

"Spill it, Pop, so we can watch it work."

"Nary a word—if she fizzles, visit us in jail. If she don't, drink hearty when this battle cry of freedom has give way to peace on earth from here to Bordeaux."

Early in the afternoon of the following day, when he had secured the Loot's car on the strength of a promise that the big Joan of Arc campaign was at last drawing to a close, old Pop Sibley and Chuck, accompanied by Jugger and Isadog, rolled to Bordeaux from the Gang's camp in the dismal swamp.

They went through Bordeaux without stopping, and after the stone bridge across the Garonne had been passed they headed straight for Izon. After one brief but copious slug of cognac in the back room of the inn at Izon, they proceeded to the house at the edge of town where their trophy had been discovered and where the statue of the heroine, minus her horse, awaited whatever events the future might add to her checkered career.

Not so large as a ship's figurehead, somewhat larger than a cigar store Indian, the figure, carved in wood, had been executed in three sections and a sword. The statue came apart at the waistline. The sword arm, uplifted, was attached to the torso by three rusty screws, but these yielded presently to Chuck's mechanical talents and within half an hour after their labors began the quartet had the heroine packed compactly in the tonneau of the Dodge.

"That's that," Pop Sibley observed. "Lay that blanket over that statue. Better put that long sword in the back seat."

When this was done, "When do we eat?" Isadog inquired. "How about them rations you mentioned, Pop?"

"Boy, don't you take no chances and eat on a empty stummick. It's mighty apt to spoil your voice. We got some visitin' to do before we eat."

A stirrup cup at the inn, and then the party journeyed back to water level by way of San Loubes and Genimont. The latter camp, which had sheltered them months before when they first arrived in France, was alive now with troops waiting to return to the United States.

Evidences of intense military discipline were visible on every hand, and the old-timers in the Dodge shivered with apprehension and breathed deep sighs of relief when they were clear of its perils. "Let's git where they ain't so many military soldiers and have a drink."

"There is soldiers every place. Git into the back room of the joint at Lowzac and it'll be safe enough."

In this sanctuary, after an hour had passed, "Allay, you birds!" Pop Sibley ordered. "It's gittin' late. We're gonna eat at Gruber's."

Entering the Dodge, "Isadog, this fog is pretty damp. You better sit up in the front seat with Chuck so you won't catch cold. Go easy on them cigarettes. You don't want your voice to git husky for a while yet."

With the Dodge and its cargo parked in front of the restaurant, the quartet dined leisurely at Gruber's.

At nine o'clock Isadog looked at his watch. "Pop, hadn't we better get goin'?"

That Ain't No Lady 245

"Take it easy and don't git nervous. We only got ten minutes' work up at the Double-track Tunnel before the big play begins, and we don't want to start nothin' till ten o'clock. Accordin' to MacFlinty's new rules, his M. P.'s don't bother you till after ten o'clock. Take it easy. Ask Alexander to encore the coonyak."

At twenty minutes before ten the quartet resumed their journey. Leaving the brighter traffic lanes, Chuck drove through dark streets until he came to the house under which lay the vaulted cavern which early in the game had been christened the Double-track Tunnel.

"You birds wait here in the car for me," Pop Sibley directed as he climbed out on the narrow sidewalk, "and for the love of the holy old goldfish don't git premachoorly pinched while I'm inside. I won't be more'n ten minutes. If the M. P.'s prowl up, tell 'em you're waitin' fer a quartermaster general. They can't pinch you now anyhow for ten minutes yet, and I'll be back by that time."

After a quick inspection and a word of greeting from the vigilant guardian at the outer door, Pop Sibley was admitted to the establishment, where, all night long, a slightly artificial Bacchanalia did the best it could to forget the cash register.

Midway of a long dark hallway Pop Sibley encountered a shriveled female member of the kitchen detail. "Listen, cheery," he said, handing the woman a five-franc note, "tell Miss Madeleine to venay ici toot sweet."

Of a certainty and with great pleasure. The brave one, meanwhile, would remain where he was?

"Ah oui, ah oui, I will rest ici," Pop answered, listening to a muffled tumult which lifted from the cavern of gayety deep below the street level.

Following her guide, a moment later Madeleine appeared in answer to old Pop Sibley's summons. "What a pleasure to greet again one of the long-absent Engineers! And the others—your brave associates?"

"All the time bokoo work, Madeleine. By and by mebby we come back. Listen, cheery, here's fifty francs." Then, lapsing into pidgin English: "I likee ketchum your coat, savvy? You lend me your coat to-night for theater show us boys is giving, and we bringum back next week. I likee ketchum one lady coat, one hat for lady actress in show."

Madeleine remembered the early days of the Battle of Bordeaux and expressed her sympathy for the enterprise. "Of a surety you may borrow my coat and my hat." She left Pop Sibley standing in the dark hallway, and returned a moment later with a scarlet cloak and a woman's hat from which burst a brilliant cerise explosion of ostrich plumes. "Voilà, mon ami."

"Bokoo mercy, Madeleine. Them are swell. Next week you ketchum."

"Any time, at your pleasure. I have others."

"Baw swaw, cheery," Pop said, bowing with some ceremony. "Us boys sure miss you and your friends. Mebby this dang war will straighten out so we can have some more parties sometime. Bong noor, cheery."

Retreating back down the dark hallway, Pop Sibley surveyed the street though the loophole in the outer door. Finding his way clear, he crossed the sidewalk in two steps and climbed into the Dodge. "Isadog, git in the back seat here with me! Jugger, you sit up there with Chuck from now on."

When the exchange had been made, "Drive up the street till you come to a dark place," the master of events directed. The car stopped for two minutes in a dark section of the narrow street, and then in response to Pop Sibley's command Chuck headed around two corners and started for the center of town.

Under a flickering light Isadog looked at his wrist watch. "Five minutes after ten," he announced. "Curfew has rang. We're on our way—where do we go from here?"

"Head fer the Green Cat," Pop Sibley ordered. "They'll be lots of the MacFlinty hornets in front of that joint. Hook that side curtain so the light can't shine so strong into the back seat. Isadog, you and Jugger hit up 'Sweet Adeline' so as to finish it just as we land in front of the Green Cat. Then start

That Ain't No Lady

'Madelon'—and don't fergit to bear down heavy on the femme voice. All set. Start the music. When the pinch comes let me do the talking."

Singing. "Yoo-re the eye-deal of my heart ... Sweet Ad-O-line." Pause. More singing. Now a shrill feminine voice broadcast the listening world with items relative to Madelon. Patrons of the Green Cat, and other inmates, sat up and took notice. From the sound of the vocal offering outside of the Green Cat, here were two or three birds whose hunt for trouble had ended in an overwhelming success. "Mebbe they ain't soldiers!" Disappointing thought. "Mebbe they're officers like us."

"They're soldiers and soused—and S. O. L. as hell!"

A stampede for the exit of the Green Cat ensued, led by the younger officers. "This gonna be a grand show. Big event!"

When the commissioned spectators got to the sidewalk the first act was well under way. An M. P., leading six of his fellow sleuths, had dived for the Dodge and the inquisition was doing fine under the leadership of the military Chesterfield. "What outfit you birds from?"

Pop Sibley went on record with a statement of fact.

"What the hell you doin' this far from home at this time of night?"

"What time is it?"

"Nix on that stuff. Who's that femme what was leadin' all youse Caruso guys?"

"She wasn't doing no singing. She isn't——"

"The hell you say! Lissen—you're pinched! You're all pinched and so is the femme." The leader of the local reform movement stepped to the running board of the Dodge and from this vantage point he issued a few orders. To a pair of his accomplices, "Git the Major on the 'phone and tell him I'm taking this mess to the Casino. This femme stuff is mighty raw,—just what he was roaring about yesterday. Ask him to come down to jail and deal the cards f'r this layout." To Chuck, "Head f'r the hoosegow, you. Casino de Lilas,—you know where it is, and you'll know it a lot better before mornin'."

On the way to the Casino, between lamp-posts against which Chuck did his best to pulverize overhanging sections of his conductor's anatomy, the M. P. did some thinking. Once his captives were delivered to the Casino much of the personal credit for the capture would be lost. The thing to do was to turn them over to Major MacFlinty without employing any middlemen. No agents. Direct to consumer. Here was the important Test Case which the unpopular police organization had hungered for. This might make history—with a promotion for the Vigilante who had engineered it. Enlisted men, using official transportation and rioting around with a female. The M. P. announced himself to the sentry at the Casino. "I've sent for the commanding officer. These are hard birds and I'll hold 'em right here in the car until the Chief looks 'em over."

A burst of high-pitched laughter from the lady in the Dodge ended in a wild shriek and a maudlin chatter of French epithets whose venom fairly shriveled the quivering ostrich plumes on her borrowed hat.

"Git calm, you! Youse guys in the back seat wid that dame—make her shut up!"

Orders is orders. Singly, and then working together, Pop Sibley and Isadog tried to quiet the feminine cyclone seated between them in the back seat of the Dodge. "Whoa, mon cheery," Pop requested in a gentlemanly tone, and then, at the top of his lungs in a stentorian mob rumble that roused lots of folks in Southern France, "Whoa, woman! In your hour of ease, on-sartain toy, and hard to please, the boys in blue were striving, upon the burning deck, put down that knife, you coward, they'll be no strike to-night, help, help, grab her neck, choke her!"—to all of which, from Jugger and Chuck, there came an accompaniment of snarls and yowls, while high above the din the shrill voice of the lady raged in the sulphuric soprano of an agitated cougar.

The crowd of assorted spectators rallied nobly.

Then, under Chuck's masterful control,

the Dodge backfired a carbon-clouded salute, and while reserve M. P. forces trotted up with their side arms for action, down the street in his limousine came the hard-boiled master of military law and order—"Mac-Flinty the Major, who made you be good."

"O-ten-shun! Gangway there, you men!" The M. P. who had made the capture in the Test Case shifted a little scenery. A brief interrogation of his good and faithful servant, and Major MacFlinty had the situation well in hand. "Get those men out of that car! Get that woman out of that car—check 'em in to the recording sergeant. What these men? What outfit they from? What that woman's name? Get her out here! Sergeant, that woman got a record?"

"What's that dame's name, youse? Get her out here!" ordered the gentlemanly M. P.

"Just like I been tryin' to tell you," Pop Sibley answered in a mild and soothing voice, "They's no lady with us a-tall. She's only——"

"I'll say she's no lady,—tell the Major what

her name is. Get her out here. Line up! Come to attention! What's that dame's name?"

A feminine voice seemed to answer the last question as the lady in the back seat of the Dodge spoke her name.

Isadog climbed out of the car and stood at attention beside his three companions.

"Get that woman out here!" The Major repeated his command in a voice that got action. Three active M. P. heroes, striving to please, dived for the curtained section of the Dodge. "Look out she don't stick you—some of 'em carry knives . . . come out here, you! Venny, toot sweet!"

The leading investigator grunted. Then he woofed like a bear. He backed out of the Dodge, bulging his two confederates behind him. The startled expression on his twisting countenance set into a mask of good hard military disguise. "Sir," he said, saluting Major MacFlinty, "there is nothing but a wooden statue in that car!" The M. P. seemed to go into a trance. He looked at his feet. "But she was singin' and raisin' hell an' wrasslin' with them two birds," he muttered. "Jeese! Mebbe I'm cuckoo!"

"What's all this? What do you mean?" The Major addressed the world.

Now the M. P. was talking to himself, and here was Pop Sibley's cue. "Sir, that statue is a Joan of Arc antique we boys was getting as a token of appreciation for a man who sent us a carload of candy and the female costume is for a female part in a show we boys are giving Sunday night and I put that cloak around that statue to keep the rain off as these raincoats are like a fish net and rain is mighty apt to swell up a wood statue and it wouldn't hurt the cloak because the show is about a poor ragged woman to keep up us Engineers' morale now that they is no more passes issued to town and——"

"What outfit?" the Major interrupted, looking sour, and planning a retreat before the impending salvo of derision might shoot his dignity out from under him "Where you men from?"

Pop Sibley was specific in his reply.

"Well—get back to it."

"Major, yessir! And would the Major kindly indorse us boys' passes so we won't git arrested on-root to destination?"

"O. K.—MacFlinty—to midnight" was the indorsement which created souvenirs of the memorable occasion.

"The Major was betwixt a laugh and busting us for life," Pop Sibley explained to the Loot on the following day. "But he acted mighty genteel."

"Which makes my painful duty all the more painful," the Loot commented, resuming work on an epistle destined to reach the desk of the Base Commander,—and to get results. The results, affecting the enlisted personnel of the Base, excited the Gang's favorable and enthusiastic comment.

"Hot dam, soldier! Read that new order! All-night passes and no M. P. trouble unless you start it!"

"Hooray f'r us Rabble,—me f'r Bordeaux Sunday night and bokoo grand times f'r me and my gal!"

"Hold the deal, wild man. Sunday night, Gang, the least us Rabble kin do is to attend the show right here in camp in a body," Pop Sibley interposed. "One and all goes to that show as a compliment to Isadog—th' best female imitatin' ventrilikist in this man's army! How about it?"

"I'll tell the cockeyed world, includin' M. P.'s, we'll be there with bells on! That bird saved us boys' life. Him and that Joan of Arc heroine licked the M. P. army single-handed and never fired a shot. Never mind the guard—drink hearty!"

Chapter 8

As You Wuz!

THE Quartermaster smiled a smirk, We won the War, you won the Work,"— and thus sang a shivering sergeant, prowling after coal in the swamps near Bordeaux while they dealt him out of a couple of poker hands in the non-com's private palace.

Detected in the theft,—"There will be—no more coal—issued to-night," the sergeant learned from the deliberate lips of the vigilant guardian of the entire A. E. F. "That's the way he acted, ennyhow," the culprit explained to his fellows. "Like the king of the world. Caught me with the goods and he like to scalp me. Told me to see my sooperior ossifer and get a proper requisition to-morrow after the banks open and everything. Me and him and the coal pile standing there in the rain, and that's the end of *that* little drammer of a hero's life."

"Damn if it is." A heavy loser realized that the game stopped when the fire went out. "See if the light's still burnin' in the Loot's shack?"

It was. Presently through the drizzling rain the harsh quartermaster was lured away from his quarters. The Loot needed help from a talented brother officer with a terribly involved bit of bookkeeping involving commutation of quarters for a horse. "Suppose you charge room and bath on your pay voucher for the horse and the horse don't take a bath—then the guv'ment sends you to Leavenworth for ten years. That's probably how the Loot kep him figgerin' so long. How much coal you birds salvage?"

"Plenty to last this hut till pay day. Then by the holy old goldfish I'm goin' to Bordeaux and drink me bokoo warming flooids until spring gits here."

"Don't talk that way. Say something cheerful about goin' home. We got here first, —you'd think they'd turn us loose sometime!"

"Lissen—we got three stripes now and the way it looks we're going to git three more before they blow the ree-call for this Gang. Only way you can get an honorable discharge is out of the barrel of some sentry's gun. Jimmy the Ink says there's a new order out for to-morrow where a lot of us hired help build a new flock of barracks for the police force in Bordeaux. Lot of new M. P. guys comin' in to help the shock troops on the coonyak beat."

"Hell again! Right when we got 'em all tame they switch the cut."

"Cheer up, you shroud—if we ketch that barracks job them new M. P. bulls'll be fraternal enough to use 'em bokoo pleasant when we need 'em. Looks pritty from where I sit. Rather build barracks in town than freeze to death in this swamp. Wonder how come that all the brains in the army always pick the soggy spots of sunny France for us swamp angels to roost in? Why can't they stick a camp up on a hill once in a while?"

"Deal me four cards,—mostly aces. Them

healthy camps is reserved f'r prisoners de guerre."

"Prisoners de garbage. Kin you beat pair queens?"

"Nuk. Not with Johns. Stoke that stove,—place is getting cold."

While the place got cold, and after the non-com's game had broken up, a light still burned in the Loot's quarters. The Loot was planning a few moves calculated to keep home happy in the face of a spreading realization that the Gang was not scheduled for a return to the United States until a lot more weeks had turned into months. The Armistice. A rotten winter. An epidemic of imported Uplifters. Step by step the Loot reviewed his mental progress chart of the Gang's morale. A bad winter bringing shriveled dispositions and a soggy outlook garnished with vinegar. The artificially promoted campaign of stepping out and into the mirth and laughter of Life in a Great City. Phony, and followed by the cold gray dawn. "A bad bet," the Loot reflected. "Missed my guess on that one." Then there had followed a period of mixed emotions in the Gang's collective mind out of which had evolved a terribly acute desire to get home. Back home. That was all. The gray cold days, the miserable nights, were endured, were fought and won under the inspiration of the thoughts of what home had come to mean. The Gang was tired.

"Stay within hailing distance," the Loot admonished the forty-man detail that left on the following day to begin work on the new police barracks in Bordeaux. "No globetrotting. We might make the riffle on the Old Home bet and if any good luck breaks we don't want the game gummed up by any A. W. O. L. stuff. Nothing lost, strayed or stolen when the ship sails—or it's a cinch it won't sail."

Privately and confidentially one of the old-timers in charge of the new detail questioned the Loot. "You think there's a chance of us getting out of France soon?"

"Blackie—not a chance." The Loot was honest with the inside crew. "Not a chance,—but don't act that way. Sort of up to us to set the pace. All of your outfit think the way you think. Well,—think cheerful. You got to smile for the next three months no matter if it breaks a jaw. You can bet your case clacker I'll be Johnny-at-the-rat-hole around the Embarkation Office and I'll overlook no bets. In the meantime, keep smiling if it kills you. If you don't, the Gang is sure to hatch a mess of wandering boys and, if that happens, when the time comes to leave—we don't leave! And that brings up the Badger question. Jimmy has still got the A. W. O. Louse Cawpril Badger on the rolls. Do everything you can to round him up."

"When was the last word of him, Loot?"

"Three months ago. Marseilles. Chances are that rambling weeper will be homesick for the Gang by this time. Maybe find him in the Bordeaux Underground. Look out for him and bring him in if you find him."

At noon when Blackie and the construction detail had left for the new barracks job, "Forty men gone," the Loot reflected. "Fat chance I have to hold the Gang together."

The noon mail brought another element of disintegration. It was an order affording ambitious tourists a hand-painted excuse for straying so far from the fold that the next war would still find them lost. A pass-craver got the good news from Jimmy the Ink late that night. The Loot had read the order, and after grunting his disgust had departed hurriedly for Bordeaux. Now, armed with the document and lacking negative instructions, the company clerk, striving to please, was enabled to shower down some blessings on a disgruntled boon-craver who fairly demanded a two-day pass for Bordeaux.

"Lissen. What's the big idea of the pass to Bordeaux for two days?" Jimmy demanded. "You just got back yesterday."

"No big idea except I'm fed up on this swamp and my blankets are moldy and I crave another touch of city life before I begin talkin' back to myself."

"How'd you like a couple of months in merry old England, or trailin' around here and there over France viewing points of interest?"

"Yeah—an' while you're dreamin', mark

the ticket New York, San Francisco and two or three good way stations!"

"I ain't dreamin'. There's an order come in sayin' that if anybody has a real thirst for culture he can get it. The government has gone crazy and your Uncle Sam will stake you to a trip here and there on the strength of your neglected education. Read that order. It just got here."

The grouch plowed his way through the document and a smile bloomed on his dirty face. "Great! Fix me up fer a course of oil-painted art, some place in England—can you do that?"

"Me and the Loot can do anything as long as the ink holds out. I'll sign you up for England, but keep it under your hat for another day. The Loot don't crave no mad rush right at this moment. It isn't due to break until to-morrow."

On the following day when the news of the opportunity to travel and see the world was published, a general stampede resulted.

"Looks like something over two hundred per cent of the outfit crave to spread their wings," Spike Randall complained to the Loot. "There's ninety ignorant men waitin' to sign on for the cruise toward the higher learning. You got to put a crimp in it somewhere."

"Nix on the crimp." After some quiet reflection, the Loot had changed his opinion of the school order. "Anything that breaks now to take their mind off their troubles is worth the price. If a natural-born K. P. feels that he needs a shot of art, let him go to it, is my motto. The Gang is wearing three stripes now, and they're fed up on the prospect of a couple more. That order is a life-saver. The Colonel says there isn't a chance of us going home for another six months, and you know as well as I do that six months more of this would turn the old Rabble into a high-grade bunch of raving Reds. I don't blame 'em. This lousy mess is cleaned up as far as the big job goes, and it's a case of go home or go crazy, and you can bet your tin hat that G. H. Q. knew it when they wrote that order. Nix on the objections, Spike—circulate around and boost this bet. I'm strong for it, and anybody that craves art can have my indorsement on his application and a few francs to get out of town on if he needs 'em."

"I guess I'm with you, Loot, but it still looks phony to have six hoggers, a couple of plumbers and half a dozen of the best steam-shovel men in the world, along with seven or eight more squads of railroaders, leap into biology and the dead languages. Well, there's one thing sure—when that outfit goes, our effective strength will be cut to something between a natural and box cars. I doubt if there'll be a dozen men left in the outfit here in camp."

"What of it? Suppose they all go; so much the better until the time comes to rally round and catch a boat home. You seem to have lots of grief on your mind, but if it'll cheer you up any I'll tell you that we've got not a thing to worry about at the present moment except the damned, perpetual, continued and chronic absence of one downtrod corporal by the name of Badger. Badger gets my goat. I've lived through everything else in this mad round of pleasure, but if I get hit sudden and die of some unknown mental washout, you can tell the padre and the surgeons that the victim made an ante mortem diagnosis of his case and called it acute Badgeritis. Jimmy the Ink has forged a ghost brand on that damned bird for six months now, until the theme of life's old sweet song is nothing but Badger, Badger, Badger. If you ever lay eyes on him again, rivet the leg irons—and by the way, when this stampede of art students starts out, tell 'em that the first principle of art is to locate Corporal Badger and bring him back here. The A. E. F. is all cluttered up with systematic D. C. I. stuff, and you've got to have a lily-white record before you can get on the boat. We'd feel damn funny climbin' the gangplank and gittin' throwed off just before the boat sailed because we were shy one louse Badger. Round him up if you can, and when you find him turn him over to me."

"When I find him I'm goin' to chain him to my left hind leg. He's had his run. Loot, there's one more thing—how you bettin' on the game Saturday?"

"That's a fool question—I'm bettin' on Mike, of course. There's nobody in the Navy half as good. Who'd you think I was bettin' on?"

"I'm not thinkin', only you better hang fire until the game begins. The old Mike has been mighty homesick lately. You know there's about forty of the old-timers that have been workin' in this war harder than anybody ever worked before. Mike was doin' about six men's work for a year and a half, and now that everything is slacked up and he has a chance to think it over, I'm afraid he might bust loose and play a heavyweight date with the old Demon Rum. If I know anything, he's due to pop any minute. That's why I'm telling you to make no bets on Saturday's game till you look it over after the first inning."

Late that night, before he fell asleep, the Loot devoted another tense hour to a summary of the general status of the Gang. The results of his analysis brought the realization that the one-time compact organization was busted wide open. "All shot to hell, high, wide and handsome—and this school mess adds the last final tourist touch."

The Loot saw quite clearly at that hour the misfortunes which might attend the disintegration of his outfit. He realized that no matter how good a scrap a man might put up single-handed, the residue of the A. E. F. would finally beat him. "We landed in a bunch and we stuck together. It was us against the world and we managed to win, but now—stand by for a few daily dishes of grief. I've got to turn a big trick and then pull off a snappy round-up or we're finished. The way this game lays right now, anybody can go to hell in a hand basket in fifteen minutes. If I'm not damned careful, when we sail for home half of the old Rabble will be left in France and the other half of us'll be in the brig wearing leg irons . . . well, it looks like I've got one more job ahead of me, one more big river to cross."

On Saturday Mike the Marvel staggered into the pitcher's box. The Gang lost its shirt and the Loot lost hope.

As a matter of history let it be recorded

that the last fact was fairly well covered up by the owner and proprietor thereof. No outward evidence afforded innocent bystanders any suggestion of the inner wreckage of what had been Hope Springing Eternal in the Loot's chest. Realizing his mood, the Loot was quick to begin a deliberate combat against it. "What I need," he reflected, "is a hell of a hearty laugh, for due cause and with just and sufficient reasons as its inspiration."

At the Loot's quarters a courier was waiting, with Lady Luck beside him, and the waiting pair, encountering the Loot in the Valley of Despair, presented him with the much-craved hearty laugh disguised as a Formal Order relative to the Hero Question. From the Order the Loot learned that two heroes, and only two, were to be designated for a ceremony, with trimmings, which would leave the pair festooned with evidence of their country's recognition of their spectacular heroism. The Loot summoned Jimmy the Ink. "Post this on the board," he directed. "It's an order for two of the Gang to get elected. D. S. M. for the two best men,—whoever they are. Competition is open to the enlisted personnel only. You guys better organize a camp meeting and elect your two heroes. I'll recommend whomever the Gang nominates. The medals are coming in the next mail. Don't lose 'em."

Poetic outbursts were the first result of the publication of the order. Reading the Literature on the bulletin board, one of the Gang's poets began an impromptu offering a moment after he had digested the Medal Order.

> "A Gen-e-ral in riding pants
> Rode in a lim-o-zeen
> Through all of Sunny Drizzling France
> Consuming gas-o-leen.
> And in addition to his pants
> He wore out bokoo ad-ju-tants
> Who carried medals mil-i-taire
> To pin on heroes everywhere."

"Rally round, youse guys! Listen to this poet! He's hittin' on all six. Who did Gin-e-ral give the first medal to? Lissen, you birds!"

Answering the demand the poet continued his song:

>"Gen-e-ral hollered for Company Bee
>Of the Shoveliers in old Bordeaux.
>'Festoon the Gang in their Olive Dee
>And sober 'em up as a favor to me;
>Parade that Rabble in a row,
>Then git in the clear and watch us go!'"

"O-ten-shun, Rabble!" The master of ceremonies cut in to afford the minstrel a chance to get his breath. "Who got th' first medal? G'wan wid that pome!"

>"'Private Mudd!' the General called,
>'Front and center, Private Mudd.'
>Out stepped a hero bent and bald,
>'You answered when your country called—
>Now in the name of a wart on France,
>In the name of the Home Guard Over
>   There,
>Hero! The Medal Mil-i-taire!'"

"Hooray! Speech! What did ol' Private Mudd tell ol' Gen-e-ral? What did he do when he got that there medal? G'wan wid that pome."

As You Wuz!

"Private Mudd he shook his head
And to the Gen-e-ral he said: Ko-russ!
'Take back your medal,
Take back your craw de guerre;
It wasn't no Greed for Glory
That drove me Over There.
I had a job on the railroad—
Had to work four hour a day;
I was so lazy the work drove me crazy
In spite of my overtime pay.
So I headed for France when I got the chance
Along with the Rabble Gang;
So don't try to peddle me no hero medal,
O-ooo, Take Back Your Craw de Guerre!' "

"Hot dam! Lissen to ol' Jack Burroughs ramble. What did th' ol' General do to the ol' Mudd when he flang back that medal? G'wan wid that pome!"

"The General turned red, white and blue
An' blew in a cloud of dust,
A-looking for a he-ro
With an overhanging bust.
He bellered out a loud command,
He yelled it fit to beat the band;
'Show me the man that won the War!'

So they showed him a Wildcat Stevedore.
'Private Black!' the Gen-ral called,
'Front and center, Private Black!
Attention, soldier! As you were!
Receive this Medal Mil-i-taire!' "

"What ol' stevedore boy say? Keep 'er goin'!"

"Nix. Can that stuff! Here's the Loot!"

"G'wan wid that pome. Loot likes it better'n you do.".

The Sweet Singer of Soggy France smiled confidentially at the Loot and continued the recital of the Big Festooning:

"Stevedore Black, he shook his head
And to the Gen-e-ral he said: Ko-russ!
'Take back yo' medal,
Take back yo' Mil-i-taire.
Wuzn't no Greed fo' Glory
Whut driv me "Oveh Dere,"—
Wuz jus' one wile, wile woman
Dat settled on my trail,
Jus' one wile, wile woman,
Whut almost skinned me pale;
Us took one backward look at Liz,
Den sez us, "Laff'yette, heah us is!"

Right now as a Hero I'se way below zero,
O-ooo, Take Back Yo' Craw de Guerre!' "

"Couldn't sell 'at stevedore boy nuthin',—what ol' General do when he got left in the rain with that medal? G'wan wid that pome. Loot says orate louder so he can hear better. Highball, soldier! What the General do?"

"The General turned a sickly green
And dove into his lim-o-zeen.
He pinned six medals on his pants,
And give the rest to his ad-ju-tants.
'Let's go!' sez he. 'This War is Hell!
If you're lookin' f'r heroes you're S. O. L.!' "

"Lissen—they ain't no more pome!" the poet announced. "That's as far as I'm going. There's only two medals in this event in the first place and we've issued both of 'em."

" 'Ray f'r th' pote! 'Ray f'r ol' Jack Burroughs!"

"Say it with coonyak!" With this parting suggestion the orator dived into his accustomed obscurity—leaving the Loot to struggle as best he could in a futile effort at obtaining the first chapters of the Big Medal

Pome. When the garbled versions had been straightened out, "Well, even if you can't remember all the bright gems of literature, there's one thing, Gang, that I want you to sure remember, day and night. Get Corporal Badger! That's all. Pass the word,—bring in that lost lamb. I need him!"

Spike Randall, sensing some matter of first importance in the Loot's words, engineered a confidential session with the Loot. "What's the burning words on the Badger question? You aim to play a cuff ace or something?"

The Loot looked steadily at Spike Randall for a long ten seconds, and then with the faint suggestion of a smile about the corners of his mouth, "Old-timer," he said, "I've leaned heavy on you in the pinches. Heavier than a ton of coal. We'll go down town for dinner. I've got a big play framed up and the first three cards have dropped and I've lost each bet. Tell you all about it at dinner where we can be quiet. Maybe you can spot the joker. I'm damned if I can."

In a private room at the Chapeau Rouge, when their dinner had given place to coffee worthy of the liqueur that accompanied it, the Loot spoke his piece to Spike Randall. "You swung on at the start of this game," he said, "and you've seen every move. You know the Gang better than I do, and you think just as much of 'em. You know as well as I do that the big play is to get 'em home before they start slipping,—now that the shooting is over. Well—the Colonel and the topside crew have been working night and day to get the Regiment on the sailing list and they've had zero luck. I horned in at headquarters and got the dope long before even the transport gang got it. If you know enough of those civilian clerks, and if you know 'em well enough, you've got a thirty-day lead on most of the ship news. Spike, you know the timber game and I know the steel, and both of us have been up against city councils and county courts and state commissions and all that squads-round-and-round stuff that is cooked up before some poor louse contractor picks off a big job at thirty per cent less than cost."

The Loot paused long enough to indulge himself with more coffee. "I sized up the field and I headed in," he continued. "I captured seven or eight of the brass necks that are running the transport stuff,—got 'em so we were boys together and dear old college chums. Turned a couple of hard problems over to the Queen of France at the Apollo and after she got 'em charmed their one object in life was to see us catch the next boat home. They played fair,—the orders issued twice. Like the time we were going to the front. They didn't stick. Always a hitch. Then I started in quietly on the hired hands and I took that office apart. Saw the wheels go round. Found out what made it go. Little bird with red whiskers by the name of Trailer. Maybe he's a Trailer but he leads the procession in the home-bound steamboat world. His waste basket has more high-toned autographs in it than seven of our hot-stove filing systems could burn up in a hard winter. He's king of Who's Who on the Gangplank. He's king of the works,—and I'm beat. He's got me beat."

"Did you try money on him?"

"Money—holy blue burning bunions! I

get a financial report on him from seven of the outfit in his office and he's got more money than the paymaster. Trailer the Patriot,—one of these 'give-all' guys with a mania for what he calls 'service.' Calms his patriotic ying by working ten hours a day for eighty a month. Hell, no, I didn't try money. 'Lieutenant, our best efforts shall be expended upon behalf of the organization to which you are attached'—that's his line. Orates. Burbles. And you can't touch him with any two-star officer stuff. He don't listen to generals. 'Just a humble servant of Democracy'—he let that ride one day."

"How about a little rough stuff,—cut his throat or something? Stop long enough to let him sign the order for a boat to haul us home, then finish the job? I don't mean goin' that far, of course,—but how about a few promises of joys to come?"

"Then we're done. Spike, you've got the same shriveled brain that's afflicted me for the past six months. You're a dud."

"How about the Queen of France?"

"Tried it. Zero."

Spike Randall yawned elaborately. "You seem to tire me out. That's the extent of my bag of tricks,—except one little sequel to the sad story. If I ever meet the bird, just on general principles I aim to take a crack at him in public and explain to the M. P. that gaffs me that the Trailer patriot with the red whiskers was cussing the police force of the A. E. F."

"You'll never get the chance. Beginning to-morrow morning Mister Trailer bumps up against the last card in my frazzled deck. Unless everything blows up, the Trailer guy surrenders to the Medico gang not later than Saturday next. Absolutely under your skull and locked up for the next ten years, I've got Doctor Jimmy enlisted. He's probably the keenest single-handed inventor in the A. E. F., and by Saturday night Trailer the Patriot will be isolated for loathsome reasons such as smallpox or worse, as a suspect in a ward where there's only one door. If we can keep him penned up for a month it's a cinch we can handle his successor and get our name on the sailing list. That's that,—and that's the reason we've got to get our missing Cawpril Badger rounded up and checked in for the last muster and hog-tied to about three squads of watchdogs. That's all. Want to go over to the Apollo for an hour? Say hello to the Queen and watch the show for a while and then beat it for the hard-earned hay? How's it sound?"

"Fair enough. Wait a second,—stirrup cup." From a bottle of brandy older than his grandfather Spike Randall poured two drinks. "Gonna absorb these like they were plain likker instead of priceless perfumery. Here's yours,—Loot, we haven't had a hell of a lot of what could be called luck for the last few months in this damn army, but I've got a hunch the first seven years are about finished. Anyhow, whichever way she breaks, here's luck!"

"Luck! . . . whuf! Come on, Devil. We've got to make our luck."

Caps and coats and a word with Madame and a message for one of the greatest culinary artists in France and then, following Spike, the Loot headed for the exit from the

Chapeau Rouge. Halfway down the long room on their way out the Loot reached forward and touched his companion's arm. "Spike! Bear a little to starboard. There's Trailer over there by the wall. Come and meet him."

"Evening, Mister Trailer; how are you? Meet Sergeant Randall. . . . Join us at the Apollo for an hour after you finish? Interesting show . . . sorry."

On the street, "Well, Spike, nobody no place never can say that you haven't viewed the Trailer remains. You can hand that down to posterity. Inside of a week he's going to be hard to see without a permit and bokoo disinfectants. Hot-looking holy bewhiskered shrimp, ain't he, to be dealing the cards for half a million home-bound tourists of the A. E. F.? Beats hell sometimes where the Eagle of Authority finds a perch."

Spike Randall mumbled his reply. After ten minutes at the Apollo he spoke clearly enough. And briefly. "Back inside of half an hour,—meet you in the Queen's dressing room. Stick here."

"Wonder what hit that bird?" the Loot mused after his companion had left. "Seemed worried about something."

Within the appointed half hour Spike Randall returned to the Apollo Theater. Following another man clad in O. D. he climbed the iron stairway backstage. "Down that way—to your left," he directed his companion. The pair halted outside of the Queen's dressing room. Spike knocked lightly on the thin door. "Loot, you at home?"

"Come on in. Where you been?"

Spike opened the door a little way. Then, with his right hand, he reached into his overcoat pocket and hauled out a mussed-up mess of red whiskers. "Tell the Queen not to get scared when——"

"What's up? Come on in. The Queen's on the stage."

At this Spike Randall kicked the door wide open. He faced the Loot. In his extended right hand he held the mangled red whiskers. Dragging along in the clutch of his left followed the long-lost Cawpril Badger. "Loot, here's your damn Mister Trailer, including his red whiskers. Badger! Help stick 'em back on him in a hurry. We got to take him to his office so he can fix up a sailing date for us and the Gang. Then off comes his phony front for good!"

The Loot stood back and took a long look at the drooping Badger. The Cawpril stood the inspection for ten seconds, and then began to whimper; at which, frowning and a bit bewildered, the Loot shook his head as if to acknowledge that here was a problem in psychology that went a mile deeper than the books.

"As you were—nix on the Niagara. Boy, if you only knew how glad I am to see you, you'd be touching off fireworks and sending floral tributes to yourself. First of all, what was the big idea in the perpetual furlough?"

"Lootenant, I liked Bordeaux so well that I couldn't bear to leave it. I met the clerk that was coming down from Headquarters to run the sailing lists. I give him a thousand dollars for his job. Then when I got to running the job I couldn't put the Gang and the Regiment on the list because I knew

Jimmy had been carrying my name on the rolls and I'd be a deserter if you sailed without me. Couldn't of stood being alone, ennyhow. I just postponed it. That's all that happened."

While the Lieutenant comforted himself with some gratifying and sulphuric language, Spike Randall pasted a few tendrils of the Badger whiskers into place. "That ain't all that's gonna happen, you louse! Lissen! You think you can get us on the list so we can sail right away?"

"Sergeant, yes, sir. I've got three or four mighty good ships on the list and you can take your pick of them."

Spike barked at the drooping captive. "Lissen, you tearful tyrant—from now on, Mister Trailer ain't nothing but a hole in the pay roll. You're Cawpril Badger, and don't forget it. One false move from now till we land safe at home and I'll kill you, and if we don't land within two weeks I'm gonna heave you overboard right where the sharks eat shrimp. Come on, you louse. Heads up! Hold your bean up while the Lieutenant pastes you in the jaw. He ought to. Hold steady before I spike you for a shroud."

Before the contemplated pasting process had developed into action, the Queen of France returned to her dressing room. Presently she became calm enough to render needed professional assistance with the prodigal Badger's make-up. "Ah oui, mon cheery," Spike replied to her when his chance came. "Bokoo comic, ness pah? Ah oui . . . lissen, Sister—frizzle out them whiskers, kinda. La mame chose like they was when I reaped 'em off of this louse. Ah, tray bong, tray bong. Bokoo mercy."

"Come on, Loot—we got to ride herd on this bird while he pardons us free through all the clogged-up military channels from here to Hoboken."

In the chill night, unmindful of the rain, the trio left the Apollo. They headed for Base Headquarters, where, under a dim light, Badger the Miracle Man signed the Trailer name to sailing orders important enough to eradicate a frazzled set of red whiskers, and to start the Gang toward the U. S. A.

Five days later, assembled by emergency orders, coonyak, cooties and culture all forgotten, deloused and delighted, the Gang and the Regiment sailed for home on board a ship whose passenger list had been designated within thirty minutes after the Queen of France smoothed out Mister Trailer's disguise.

Sweethearts and wives, mascots and milling creditors gummed up the Gang's departure. "The damn boat looks more like a travelin' circus with all them dogs and animals blatting around on deck."

"Never mind how the boat looks. It feels like it's headed home, and that's enough to hold me fer a while."

"Me, too . . . Jeese, I hope my first wife don't meet me and this replacement right at the dock. You suppose they can find out when we're due home?"

"Sure they can. The papers tell everything, now that there ain't no more subs. Why, what's eatin' on you?"

"Oh, nuthin' much except one of the horrors of war. Lissen—can the captain of the ship issue you a military divorce at sea like he can marry you?"

"He can't issue me none. My strings are all cut. You mean you already got one wife at home and you're takin' Clothilde back with you?"

"Yeah—anyhow she's on the boat," the culprit confessed.

"Cheer up. What's an extra wife or two among us Rabble? Turn her over to a replacement and forget it."

"Not by a damn sight. If the replacement gets anything he gets the first one. Lissen, what's the law on those subjects?"

"Ask the Loot. He'll fix it some way. Let him sign a certificate about how you got hit in the head with a box car and forgot you were already married. Leave it to him. Let Spike tell him about it."

Nearing home, when some of the problems had been solved, Jimmy the Ink got into the stretch with his overdue paper work. "Loot, what about those two medals?" Jimmy inquired. "Somebody's got to get 'em. Who draws the winning numbers?"

The Loot turned to Spike Randall, who was resting, relaxed at full length on a hatch cover beside him. "Who's elected, Spike?"

Spike sat up. Deep in his eyes burned a smile. "The polls aren't closed," he said, "but incomplete returns from one out of a coupla hundred presinks of iniquity indicate an overwhelming victory for Cawpril Badger."

"Fair enough. Jimmy, we'll pin one on Cawpril Badger right after the ship lands."

"Right,—who gets the other one, Loot?"

"Lissen, Ink. You've kept all the harrowing details off of my war-torn mind for almost two years,—don't bust your record now. Pin it on a dentist or turn it in as surplus property. Keep it if you thirst for fame,—I'll sign the fatal papers, whatever you do. G'wan aft with your problems. Spike and I are building a railroad. Allay,—but remind me about Badger and his medal right after we are safe ashore."

"Lootenant, yessir!"

While the ship was warping into the dock at the Most Glorious end of the trip, the Loot got around to a question that had bothered him for nearly two weeks. He sought Spike Randall. "For the love of the stem-winding Sherlock, tell me something, Spike. How did you spot Badger and his beard? How come you saw clear through the curly camouflage that hid Mister Trailer from this cruel world?"

Able to laugh now, Spike laughed. "Loot, you remember that hundred-year-old coonyak we finished up with at the Chapeau Rouge the night we caged the Badger Bird? Every time we had dinner together in that place we rated that ancient coonyak. I gulped it. You always hung fire and orated about how the Frogs got their money's worth out of the bouquet. Ceremony stuff. I got the big idea that night for the first time. Started me thinking about smells. Got to thinking about skid grease and cable dope and steam on cinders and wet ferns and the big timber and sour hemlock and sagebrush. Remember, the last slug we had I said, 'Here's luck!' You said we had to make our luck. Well, a minute later we fouled up on Mister Trailer and his red whiskers—and I nailed him. Hair oil. Old baldy Badger got run out of every tent in the outfit at American Lake on account of the mange cure and skunk oil and skid grease and the rest of the goo he plastered on his bean. I spiked him by the smell ten feet away before we shook hands. Had it all doped out by the time we got to the Apollo. That's all."

"Not by a cheering throng it isn't all. That beak on the front end of your map meant more to this outfit than all the imported welfare that ever hit us in the A. E. F. Come below. I salvaged a souvenir." When the souvenir was opened, and when it's century-old bouquet had filled the narrow stateroom, the Loot hoisted his glass to Spike Randall. "Old-timer," he said, "here's luck!"

"Drink hearty." . . . Whuf! . . . "Loot, we'll make the luck. Us and the rest of the Rabble got to work or starve now that this man's army is finished, but no matter how the cards drop, we'll make our luck!"

"Fair enough—we'll pin a few spans some place on the West Coast and pyramid the profits. C'mon up on deck while we see the show."

The show was quiet. There was less reality to the home-coming than there had been to the departure long months ago. Even at this hour France, to the Gang, had become little more than a half-remembered dream. The nightmare effects had vanished. "God, I'd like to get back to Bordeaux for one more day!"

The Loot's personal reverie was interrupted by an orderly bearing a message from Regimental Headquarters. The Loot read the note, and his smile became a laugh. He handed the document to Spike Randall. "Here's where all of us brass necks get unhitched out of all the fancy harness. Read it. Old Jack Burroughs at his best!"

"1. Extract from E. I. No. 13, Hqs. S. O. S., A. E. F., of January 4th, 1919, Sec. XV, Par. 1, reads *'Wearing of Sam Browne or Liberty Belts in the United States will not be permitted'* (WD Cable No. A 2293, December 7, 1918)."

"2. Therefore:

"After this date you will relegate your Sam Browne belt to the bourne
  Of useless gear, as a souvenir of the modern Samson shorn.
  We approach the strand of our own homeland; home ties must now replace
  The vested pride of the polished hide whose loop we used to grace.

"The Sam Browne belt is doomed to melt in the mists of other days
  With sword and spur and the things that were when Mars was the current craze.
  The polished strap is soon to snap like the thread of a passing dream,
  As the shore line nears and the *Texan* steers to the upraised torch's gleam.

"While we ride the swell you will bid farewell to the belt of your vested strength,
  For our work is done and the race is won by many an ample length.
  From its wonted rest at waist and chest the symbol now must fly,
  For the U. S. A. is over the way,—so bid your belts good-by."

Spike handed the order back to the Loot. "Looks like the Home Guard is jealous. You see the date—that order was written four days ago. Also looks like Headquarters was afraid to spring it on you until we landed. What are you doin'?"

The Loot had dropped his Sam Browne belt over the side of the ship. "Never mind what I'm doin'. Some things get tighter than handcuffs. Listen . . . there goes the bugle—round up the Rabble,—we're going ashore!"

There were no brass bands on the dock. Soldiers were old stuff. "We sneaked out and we snuk back."

Somebody had remembered, however, for at the shore end of the gangplank a reception committee of eight old ladies, bearing gifts, met the Rabble Shoveliers.

One of them thrust an orange at the Loot with a threatening gesture as he came ashore with the Gang. The Loot expressed his gratitude with a quick bow. Accepting the gift, he smiled at the little old lady.

The three gold stripes on his arm caught

his eye. Once they had been as brightly yellow as the orange, but now their brilliance had faded.

The orange seemed to be softer than an orange should be. The Loot pressed it gently with his thumb. Sure enough, the orange was rotten.

He handed it to Corporal Badger, who marched out of step near him. "Here's a present for you," the Loot said. "Reward of virtue. I've got a medal for you, too. Remind me about it when we hit camp."

THE END